Ways of Understanding and Education

Studies in Education   ISSN 0458-2101

A series of monographs published by Heinemann Educational Books for the Institute of Education, University of London. Other titles in the series:

Studies in Education (new series) 18

Ways of Understanding
and
Education

Louis Arnaud Reid

HEINEMANN EDUCATIONAL BOOKS
for the Institute of Education, University of London

Heinemann Educational Books Ltd
22 Bedford Square, London WC1B 3HH

LONDON   EDINBURGH   MELBOURNE   AUCKLAND
HONG KONG   SINGAPORE   KUALA LUMPUR   NEW DELHI
IBADAN   NAIROBI   JOHANNESBURG
PORTSMOUTH (NH)   KINGSTON

British Library Cataloguing in Publication Data
Reid, Louis Arnaud.
   Ways of Understanding and education.—(Studies
   in education. New series, ISSN 0458-2101; 18)
   1. Education—Philosophy—1895–
   I. Title   II. Series
   370′.1   LB1025.2
ISBN 0-435-80884-2
ISBN 0-85473-240-3 Institute of Education

Filmset by Fakenham Photosetting Ltd, Fakenham, Norfolk
Printed and bound in Great Britain by
Biddles Ltd, Guildford and King's Lynn

Note on the Author

Louis Arnaud Reid is Professor Emeritus of Philosophy of Education in the University of London. He held the Chair of Philosophy of Education at the Institute of Education from 1947 until 1962.

He was born at Ellon, Aberdeenshire, in 1895, the son of a minister, and began his studies at the University of Edinburgh in engineering. On the outbreak of war in 1914 he volunteered for the army and joined the Royal Engineers. By this time he had already taken up the philosophical studies which were to be the enduring passion of his life. So when he returned to the University of Edinburgh after being invalided out of the army it was to philosophy, rather than the practical career on which he had earlier embarked. He gained a first class honours degree in Mental Philosophy in 1919 and was awarded several University medals and prizes.

He was appointed Lecturer in Philosophy at University College Aberystwyth in 1919 and held the post until 1926. After appointments as Visiting Professor at Stanford University, California, and Independent Lecturer in the University of Liverpool, he became Professor of Mental and Moral Philosophy at Armstrong College (now the University of Newcastle upon Tyne) in 1932, a post which he held until he moved to the London Institute of Education in 1947.

Professor Reid's previous publications include *Knowledge and Truth: An Epistemological Essay*, 1923; *A Study in Aesthetics*, 1931; *Creative Morality*, 1936; *Preface to Faith*, 1939; *The Rediscovery of Belief*, 1945; *Ways of Knowledge and Experience*, 1960; *Philosophy and Education*, 1961; and *Meaning in the Arts*, 1970.

Professor Reid is Life-President of the Philosophy of Education Society of Great Britain. In recent years his major interest has been in thinking about the arts and their role in education, but he has been remarkably consistent over more than sixty years in maintaining the holistic view of which this book is a reaffirmation. At the age of ninety he still teaches regularly in the Department of Art and Design of the University of London Institute of Education.

Contents

Foreword
Harold Osborne

I have known Louis Arnaud Reid for more than three decades and, like so many others, I have been constantly amazed by the alertness and vitality with which he has pursued his chosen course. As the years pass I have become more and more impressed by the importance of the point of view for which he stands, and I am proud to have called him my friend. I read the script of this book with pleasure and respect, for in it is encapsulated the insight which is peculiarly his own, and I am honoured to be asked to write a Foreword to it.

The conventional division of mental functions into perceiving, feeling, willing, emotion and reason is convenient for those who write and read textbooks of psychology, but all such compartmentalizations break down before the concrete occasions of life. The human mind is an undivided whole and in all our contacts, however arcane, it is the mind as a whole that responds. However abstruse or impersonal be the subject of attention, there is always an underlying feeling that attention is—or is not—worthwhile. And it is feeling not reason which creates our sense of value. So, too, knowledge is not restricted to the sort of abstract awareness which can be verbally formulated and communicated in discursive discourse. There is direct, intuitive apprehension which supports and gives substance to all our discursive formulations. It is this which dominates our experience of other people, directs our sense of values and is cultivated in our appreciation of art and beauty. It is the inarticulate knowledge so conveyed which forms the core of personality and makes each one of us an individual rather than a cipher.

In his writing on education as in his writing on the theory of the arts, this holistic standpoint is central to Arnaud Reid's message. He is clear that the central purpose of education should be the enrichment and development of the personality as a whole, and this must include the enhancement and honing of that power of direct apprehension which can never be wholly accommodated within verbal propositions. It involves the training of sensibility, the maturation of feeling and emotion, with the power of judgement that these bring with them. As Sir Herbert Read in his day maintained that our education errs on the side of excessive verbalization, so Arnaud Reid opposes the exaggeratedly rationalistic conception of education propagated by some contemporary philosophers of education in favour of his own holistic ideal of personality. This carries with it rejection of the 'utilitarian' bias of our present national education policy in favour of the contrasted ideal of 'the nourishment and development of the human spirit' and of 'the values by which the spirit lives and has its being'.

This is an old man's book, a book that speaks the wisdom of long and cumulative experience in a spirit ever young and fraught still with the vitality of youth. In this respect I can compare it only with Etienne Souriau's *La couronne d'herbes*. Its message is respect for the human spirit, for the values which make men human, and it is lit by a burning sense of the importance of education. Beneath the argument and controversy one is always aware of the dedication which is its inspiration.

If we owe any duty at all to the future—and this after all is the whole meaning and implication of educating the young—then it is our duty to work for the continued progress of the race in sensibility, feeling and intelligence, rather than to look only for what is expected in the short term to be the most profitable in material benefits. By giving preponderance to utilitarian and materialistic aims, man cramps his own mind and nature and proceeds backwards, undoing the advances he has made. We need the inspiration of men like Arnaud Reid with insight and penetration to see the true goals of humanity.

H.O.
Rapperswil, Switzerland
November 1985

Preface

It is commonly agreed that a main aim of education is the attainment and development of knowledge and understanding. The 'knowledge' which is sought is generally assumed to be what can be expressed clearly in true propositional statements of fact, of 'discursive knowledge' about history, geography, science, economics, technology . . .

This assumption is valid, as far as it goes, and these are important fields of knowledge. But is 'knowledge', 'knowing', the 'cognitive' to be identified with this, and confined to what can be said in ordinary or other symbolic language? Surely not. We speak of knowing through sense perception, of knowing people, works of art, the morally good and bad. We speak of knowing-how. Yet we certainly cannot say adequately in clear propositional language what it is that we know and understand in these various fields. Generally speaking our knowing and understanding of such things must, at least at the outset, be based on direct, personal, intuitive experience. We can of course say many things *about* them: verbally expressed reflections upon the content of what we directly and intuitively experience can clarify and illuminate, so that, retroactively, we come to see more clearly and in greater depth what was at first impressionistic. There is an essential interplay between reflective thinking (which is discursive) and direct intuitive experiences: they need each other.

In order to understand better the interplay, not only of intuitive experience and discursive thinking, but between the various functions and aspects of mind involved—thinking, feeling, action, will—we have first to recognize clearly that there *are* various ways of knowing and understanding very different from one another, each with its own structure and form. To know and understand within mathematics, empirical science, technology, philosophy . . . exhibits one range of plurality of structures. Knowing and understanding in the spheres of art, morality, personal relationships ... exhibits another. Each way of knowing and understanding has its own form which calls for delineation.

The underlying distinction and difference between the two groups has to be clearly emphasized. The symbols mainly employed in the first group are discursive, expressed in propositional statements. The symbols of the second group—the arts, morals, interpersonal understanding—are primarily non-discursive, though discursive reflection can clarify, illuminate their content. They are realms of *value*, in which feeling, what I shall call 'cognitive feeling', plays a particularly important part.

The implications of this distinction for education and the educational curriculum is crucial. In the long history of Western culture, and in our educational curricula, 'knowledge' has been identified with its discursive propositional forms, and the curriculum not only been hugely dominated by them, but dominated largely to the exclusion of non-discursive knowledge and understanding, implying a separation of thinking and feeling. This divisiveness is, on any liberal view of education as concerned with whole persons, disastrously destructive. It is destructive in that the capacities for feeling and understanding required for the development of non-discursive awareness remain undeveloped and so wither and become atrophied.

The neglect of the arts—all the arts—is an outstanding example of the lop-sided epistemology endemic in our culture and ideas of education. It is no new thing: but the present political-materialistic ideology of our rulers is making it worse. Instrumentalist in motive and tone, it is hell-bent on widening the gap between utilitarian, 'cost-effective', studies conceived as means to ends, and the nourishment and development of the human spirit and the values by which the spirit lives and moves and has its being—and of which the arts are one feeding source. The arts and the humanities are in fact being progressively squeezed out. For long poor relations, they are now, by deliberate policy, to be given only the time left over (if any) from the studies which can be shown to be useful.

So, starved of cultural education in school, children are driven to turn to the stereotypes of the commercial media, where they are fed but not nourished.

This work, then, is a philosophical study of the structures and dynamics of the several ways of knowing and understanding and of their interactions with one another. It is written throughout within a holistic conception of the person, with its vitally important implications for the form and spirit of personal education.

The book is addressed, not only to professional educationists and to professional philosophers who may be interested, but to anyone who thinks and cares about education. The writing is clear and untechnical.

I am greatly indebted to friends and colleagues who have taken the trouble to read my typescript, which has been rewritten several times.

Klaus Neuberg scrutinized several versions and saved me from bad mistakes, particularly of form. Ray Elliott read an early draft and made penetrating and characteristically apposite comments. Leslie Perry's sympathetic understanding and criticism from first to last made it possible for the book to reach its present state.

On standards of style and form, my wife has been valiantly insistent— for which I am truly grateful. *All* my readers have justly castigated me for a bad habit of parentheses. I have cut out a lot of them. I hope to improve and in future to 'leave unnecessary stones unturned, and perhaps fewer avenues explored'!

To Alfred Harris I owe special gratitude, not only for his deep sympathy with the holistic approach of the book but also for his practical help in many ways.

Finally, warm thanks to Denis Baylis for his sensitive and perceptive co-operation as editor for the Institute of Education Publications Committee, during the work of preparing the book for press.

L.A.R.
September, 1985

Chapter I
'Knowledge', 'Language' and Personal Development

1. Knowledge divided from 'feeling'

It is widely agreed, among those who in different ways are concerned with education, that a main aim of education—some would say *the* aim of education—is the development of 'mind', and of 'cognitive understanding'. What is 'cognitive understanding' here taken to mean? Very commonly, matter of fact, 'objective' knowledge about the world we live in, the world of everyday common sense, of history, geography, the sciences. Such knowledge is dependent on the acquisition of basic skills—of language, reading, writing, counting. 'Knowledge' is knowledge *about* the world and the people who live in it, knowledge *that* things are so and so: and it is knowledge which can be expressed in words or other agreed systems of symbols.

Such knowledge, it is assumed, stands in sharp contrast to 'subjective' matters, what one feels, or feels about—private sensations, emotions, imaginings, hopes, fears, loves, hates ... and a mass of urgings or frustrations, pleasures and pains ... all mixed together in an amorphous mass of inner experiences for which we have no names. Knowledge (as described in the first paragraph) is an achievement of what we call 'mind': and it aims at being as impersonally objective, as 'neutral', as possible. This is valid as far as it goes. But if the 'mind' which 'knows' is so sharply divided from all 'subjective' experiences which are *not* regarded as 'knowledge', is this not a very arbitrary division of the personal human being into two parts, the part which 'knows', the 'mind', and another part which does not know but which only subjectively 'feels', each functioning quite independently of the other? And is not the account of knowledge just given an account of one kind of knowledge, an indisputably important kind, but yet only one kind? Are there not other kinds of knowledge, perhaps many other kinds, in which knowing is not so cut off, so sterilized, from other aspects of personal life, the life in which feeling plays an important part, and where knowing is the functioning of a person responding as a whole human being?

I believe, along with many others, that there are different ways of knowing and different kinds of knowledge and understanding. Nevertheless what may be labelled the 'impersonal' account of 'knowledge' is one which is very deeply rooted in our culture and in our conceptions of education, to the extent that nothing which does not fit into, or cannot be reduced to, the 'true-propositional-statement-form' is thought to be genuine knowledge. This reductiveness as it operates in a great deal of education is profoundly detrimental to personal development. The assumed dualism can be profoundly destructive. The life of personal subjects, the life of feelings and emotions, of the creative urges, of obscure symbolisms, of moral urges and intimations, religion, personal relations—all these, cut off, on this divisive assumption, from the critical purgings of thinking and intellect, remain raw, chaotic, often infantile. The personal self is split down the middle. The split is actively cultivated and deepened by the commercial forces which have espoused a mindless mass-culture and the media as a glorious source of profit.

This is a huge issue, with a large literature, both on the historical origins and development of the division through the centuries, its contemporary influences on present culture and educational attitudes and curriculum. In this book, of necessarily limited range and subject matter, I have to resist the temptation, in a brief introduction, even to begin to enlarge upon it. I can only refer to familiar facts, arbitrarily itemizing some particular high points in the historical story, and pointing to the existence of contemporary writings by social anthropologists and educationists, and of government reports.

Historical items go back to Plato, for whom reason, and particularly mathematical reason, was supreme, the senses deceptive, the arts not knowledge, though affecting character and the emotions for good or ill. The rationalist Descartes, 'father of modern philosophy', conceiving of himself as a 'thinking substance', in love with 'the mathematics', mind cut off from body and all extension, pronounced their truths alone to be objective, all else obscure and confused. On the train of the dominating triumph of science and mathematics in the seventeenth century, poetry no longer expressed deep truths, but 'cozened' feelings, was for 'fancy' and pleasure, a delightful 'fiction'. For the God of religious experience was substituted a rationalist deism, postulating a wholly transcendent

God indifferent to human cares. The concern of the empiricists in their turn was not with 'experience' in any holistic sense but chiefly with sense experience and again 'the mathematics' as a check and standard. Hume's often quoted pronouncement sums up much of a long prevailing conviction: 'If we take in our hand any volume, of divinity, of school metaphysics, for instance, let us ask, does it contain any abstract reasoning concerning quantity or number? No. Does it contain any experimental reasoning concerning matter of fact and existence? No. Commit it then to the flames, for it can contain nothing but sophistry and illusion.'[1] This is of course absurdly simplified. The sharp division between what is firmly thought to be knowledge and knowledge-seeking, which is 'objective', and the subjective which is not 'knowledge', goes very deep.

Because of it, and because of the general consensus that the main aim of education is 'cognitive' development, it is to be expected that the 'cognitive', understood in this way, should occupy nearly all of the school curriculum, and particularly in the later years of school. And so it is. Here again there is a body of material from various sources which not only shows what this proposition generally has meant, but also how there are powerful governmental forces working against what I have so far (adopting the common jargon) called the 'subjective' elements in education, including notably the arts—supposedly functions of the emotions. The facts are well known. I will here only quote comments from three sources on the position of 'the expressive arts' in the curriculum.

Peter Abbs writes:

> The expressive arts in this country, as in all modern technocracies, lie on the very fringe of the school curriculum. One can be certain that each child in our schools will be frequently and formally exposed to the symbolic systems of mathematics, physics, chemistry, geography, history and literature, but there is no certainty that in the course of his school life he will be exposed in any systematic way to the expressive disciplines. There is no assurance that any child will master a musical instrument or learn to make music; there is no assurance that he will have experience of making plays or films; no assurance that he will have opportunities to write his own poems and songs; no certainty that he will have the chance to make pottery, tapestries, sculpture and so forth. It is true that the child will do some art—painting and drawing—but at Primary School this will probably be unguided and undemanding decoration or copying, and at the secondary level it will probably comprise one hour a week and become optional in the third or fourth year. Of course, there are exceptions, but I am seeking to describe the general pattern.[2]

From the *Bullock Report*:

> It would seem that 42 per cent of nine-year olds do no drama in the classroom. If it were suddenly discovered that 42 per cent of our children did no mathematics at nine, there would be a national outcry. But why is mathematics assumed to be of such importance and drama of so little consequence? Why are the expressive disciplines at the edge of the school curriculum?[3]

Malcolm Ross, writing of a government-issued report, *A Framework for the Curriculum* (1980) remarks:

> With the curious exception of literature the arts don't figure among the subjects reserved to the core of the curriculum. Although the words 'aesthetic' and 'creative' appear on page 3 as, together, constituting one of the eight areas of experience with which the curriculum should be concerned, the reader has to wait until the last page . . . for the subjects usually thought of as 'the arts' to receive a specific mention. The section that includes the arts (along with craft, design, technology, history, geography, careers, moral and health education, etc., etc.) is headed 'Preparation for adult and working life'—from which one draws certain conclusions about their perceived educational function. Schools, so the document observes, will be under intense pressure and the none-core subjects will have to be fitted in as best as possible, perhaps in special topics taught in short courses, perhaps allowed some scope within the teaching of the core subjects. However—indeed whether—the arts figure, their lowly status is made perfectly clear.[4]

2. Effects on the person; mass-culture

I have so far merely illustrated one effect of a traditional, and current, interpretation of the word 'knowledge'—as what we can intelligently say in reasoned, objective, truth-claiming statements. Such 'knowledge' does not, as we said, apply to the experiencing and expressions in which feelings are influential operators. The educational curriculum is almost entirely taken up with the first to the virtual exclusion of the second.

But to confine the expression of knowledge to one type, the propositional-statement type, is to deprive children of a major part of their heritage. In order to come to know more fully in different ways, we have to learn to express in different ways, for each kind of knowing has its own medium of expression. If we refuse the opportunities for this experiment and learning, we are cutting off the potentialities of human development, of powers to discover new ranges of meaningful experience. So deprived, the potentialities will wither and die, will atrophy, as certainly as if the eye were deprived of light, an arm prevented from movement, a child cut off from human speech.

This is what, to a large extent, is actually happening. I will not apologize for quoting Peter Abbs once again: he puts it eloquently in his *Reclamations*. He shows how, in the absence of cultural education in schools the starved emotions of children are turned from the 'neutral' school to the media of personal culture where they are bombarded, without much choice, by the products of commercial mass-culture. It is to be seen

> in the newsagents [where] the highly popular magazines for adolescent girls, which bind cosmetics, fashion, pop-music and romance into one dreamy gestalt, proliferate. At the local cinema one can see the endless sequences of 'X' films they view. Add to the magazines and films, BBC1, ITV and BBC2 television, the recordings of 'pop hits' on disc and cassette, and, behind these, the all-pervasive influences of advertising and publicity, and we have a crude map of the commercial culture to which the great majority of adolescents are deeply and uncritically attached . . . I am suggesting that there is a rift in our society between knowledge and passion, between fact and ritual, which we must become aware of and come to terms with. Given this rift, it is not altogether surprising that the adolescent, even the intelligent adolescent, sees learning as a dull, if necessary, activity and commercial culture as colourful, ritualistic, releasing; not surprising that after the day's routine at school he returns home to play the latest music full-blast; not altogether surprising that he assumes that it is the glossy products of mass-culture and not the studies at school which embody the quintessential rhythms and inner purposes of life itself.[5]

The mass-culture is not *folk*-culture, expressing essentials of life, initiation, marriage, death, work, people in relationship.

> The content of most pop songs would seem to be, significantly, confined to adolescent dream-sexuality, and here too the songs are invariably vague, stereotyped and, in truth, more infantile than adolescent ('baby, baby, baby') . . .

We find love as an abstraction rather than the actual loving of a person as a being in the world.

> [It] is the same unreal love, sentimental, evasive, stereotyped, that we find week after week in the teenage magazines which litter the shelves of our newsagents. In true culture we invariably find a high degree of specificity, a strong sense of context, of time and location, a sense of unique relationships, of binding existential meanings; in false culture we tend to find the reverse, we find a high degree of generality in which all things prickly, problematic and diverse have been conveniently dissolved.[6]

It is clear, then, that in personal education it is extremely important that children should have ample opportunities for exploring new, intrinsic and specific values and meanings for themselves, and to make these specific and real by, in various ways, expressing them. In these explorations and expressions the arts have a vital part to play. The insights we can have in and through them, the aesthetic experiences they yield, as well as the aesthetic sensitivity they develop for unlimited experiences outside the arts, give them a position of central importance in education and in life outside it.

3. Concepts, language, and spiritual asepsis

'Knowledge', in the conventional view, is tied up with statements. I want now to say something, provisionally, about language and its relation to the formation of concepts and propositions.

It is very widely held that human thinking is inseparable from its *linguistic* expression. There is undoubtedly a sense in which, at certain levels of discursive thinking, this is true. (The present discourse is doing it all the time.) Through it science and philosophy become possible. What is usually understood by 'conceptual thinking' is of this kind. But the concepts here involved do not suddenly spring into perfect being with the utterance of language, or other conventional symbols. They are derived, ultimately, from sense perception and imagination. Different senses automatically pick out—in a way, 'make'—different qualities, sound, colour, touch, etc. Natural perceptual development, pre- and post-linguistically, includes, in its early stages of development, classification and the relating of qualities. Before babies learn to use language, they distinguish between yellow and blue, a ball from a cube, and recognize, without naming them, likenesses and differences. A little later, with pride and joy, they learn to name them, thus fixing them in the mind. 'Yellow' is different from 'blue', the several balls or cubes are 'like' one another. As we observe this development, we may say that they recognize 'conceptual' characters and relations between different things. But of course the word 'conceptual' has different meanings at different stages of development, and it is too easy to jump too quickly from a very simple and primitive sense of the term to a very sophisticated one. In one sense the baby, in perceptual discriminating and relating, is 'thinking conceptually'. But if that is true it has, quite obviously, a different meaning from the process which is going on when a mathematician or scientist or philosopher is 'thinking conceptually'. Babies' 'conceptual thinking' (in a rather more sophisticated sense) develops when they begin to use words and explicit sentences. To name this 'red' and that 'blue' is but a stage towards conceiving 'redness', 'blueness' . . . 'colour', 'shape', and to the use of these and other words in adult speech of discursive complexity. Learning to think is a continuous process of development: it is quite artificial to think of it in layers, to say babies do not 'think' or 'know' until they have mastered the use of abstract language.

When abstract language has been learned, what does it do? It is a familiar platitude that it releases us temporarily, and as a phase of thinking, from preoccupation with particulars and individuals. The picking out and verbally (or otherwise symbolically) articulating of characters of particulars which resemble characters of other particulars, or, as we often say, are 'common' as between particulars, enables us to generalize them, to make general statements covering an indefinitely large class of qualities, without having to refer to particulars. The words 'red', 'spherical' refer to the 'redness' and 'sphericity' of all red or spherical particular objects, without our having to look at or cite them. So discursive languages, with their unlimited ranges, become possible. Another aspect of this is that the symbolic language used is established by convention and governed by agreed syntactical rules, and so is *public*. But abstractions, being general, necessarily leave out nearly everything experienced. My experience of a red, round tomato is not, as a bit of perception, simply of 'red' and 'round', but, as my personal experience, a concrete experience of (say) this tomato on this plate, fragrant, juicy-looking, tempting me to eat, calling up delightful anticipatory images of the enjoyment of eating a good ripe tomato. The word 'tomato' is general, public, and as a general word, impersonal. And so used, it is emancipated from all my individual personal enjoyments of it, and in the context of general language is a coin for common discourse—with all the benefits and advantages of that discourse. So, abstract language is a great release; and that is a main function of it. It opens the way to an unlimited range of one indispensably important kind of language.

To emphasize the point: if this is a release, it is a temporary release, and one *phase* of thinking and knowledge. Abstract thinking is *abstract* thinking, in that it uses language which picks out from a concrete particular experience which is prior to it, from which it is, as a phase, temporarily detached, but can never be totally emancipated. (Pure logic and mathematics are exceptions.) Discursive, for example scientific, language can, it is true, for long run along its own rails without reference back constantly to images and particular examples. But its abstraction is originally from particulars and in the end must come back to particulars. This abstractionist view is of course disputed. Peter Geach, for example, writes: 'In the sensible world you will find no specimens of alternativeness and negativeness from which you could form by abstraction the concept of *or* or *not*.'[7] Of course it is true that 'nowhere in the sensible world could you find anything, nor could you draw any picture, that could suitably be labelled "or" or "not".' Nevertheless is it not true that highly abstract words like these, abstractions of abstractions, derive their meanings from concrete experience, perceptual or imaginal? And it is a familiar enough fact that highly abstract scientific hypotheses can have their origins in perceptual models, images and dreams. From the particular concrete experiences of prepared and trained minds they come as meaningful suggestions, and back to empirical testing, where possible, they go.

If we talk of 'release' from particulars for the sake of important discursive generalization, and of the return to particulars in exemplification, it is release bought at a price. 'Buttercup' as a class-word does not of course refer to this buttercup I see now, nor in handling this 'instance' of buttercup am I enjoying an individual buttercup as it grows in the field. A *specimen* of 'buttercup' is a different kind of creature, a conceptually created creature, different from the natural growing buttercup I see. It is a particular *instance* and not an *individual*. Of course we have to generalize, and instantiate, and in doing so we are acquiring a certain sort of knowledge and living a certain sort of life, the life of the overt conceptual knowledge and understanding of objects. But it is, as I have suggested, a phase of living. It can be a very long-lasting phase, in the sense that scientists may devote their lives to science, and do it with enduring passion. But if what is only a phase, obsessively occupies the whole of life in the inclusive sense of 'life', it can become a denial of life and of other kinds of knowing and knowledge. Abstraction is, necessarily, dessication, and if we live too long or too exclusively in a world of dessicated entities (and systems of them), if we reify them and get into the habit of assuming or thinking (as many from Plato on have done) of this as the *real* world, as the world of the only true knowledge, then another living part of us becomes atrophied. Darwin, speaking in grief of the atrophy of a part of his brain which 'seems to have become a kind of machine for grinding general laws out of large collections of fact', complains that 'for many years I cannot endure to read a line of poetry'.[8] But for this, he might have quoted Wordsworth's 'Intimations of Immortality':

There was a time when meadow, grove, and stream,
The earth, and every common sight,
To me did seem
Apparelled in celestial light,
The glory and the freshness of a dream.
It is not now as it hath been of yore;—
Turn wheresoe'er I may,
By night or day,
The things which I have seen I now can see no more.

J.S. Mill writes:

Analytic habits may ... strengthen the association between causes and effects, means and ends, but tend to weaken those which are, to speak familiarly, a *mere* matter of feeling. They are therefore (I thought) favourable to prudence and clearsightedness, but a perpetual worm both at the root of the passions and of the virtues; and above all fearfully undermine all desires, and all pleasures ... My education, I thought, had failed to create these feelings in sufficient strength to resist the dissolving influences of analysis.[9]

4. Discursive language, and languages expressing 'experience'

Analytic-synthetic discursive thinking, then, achieves its important ends by abstraction from all private and personal sensations and feelings. The dynamics of an aircraft accelerating for take-off, rising, climbing to its cruising height, can be expressed in very complex mathematical terms, supported perhaps by models, diagrams, drawings. There may be sensations and subjective feelings involved in this process of scientific or technological understanding, but they are auxiliary only, and irrelevant to the results. The *experience* of a watching observer, or passenger in the rising plane is, on the other hand, compounded of a vast complex of sensations and feelings—pressures, noise, visual experiences, organic sensations, an exciting glow of vitality tempered perhaps by a slight anxiety eased once the plane has cleared the ground obstacles at the end of the runway. The gain of technical knowledge on the one hand requires the suppression of concrete personal experience. The enjoyment of concrete personal experience can be had in total ignorance of technical knowledge—though possession of some of that may easily enhance the imaginative excitement of the experience.

But the comparison, so far, is unbalanced as between the impersonal discursive *language* of science and technology, and the concrete personal *experiences* which in the use of such language the scientist or technologist must suppress or leave out. This in itself is unfair. For in stressing, quite truly, how abstraction must leave much out, it may seem to be overlooking the fact that science and technology are *human* enterprises, that in original scientific research and discovery there is passion and exhilaration and glory, and that originative scientific work is one of the great enterprises of man. Scientific adventure is experience of major importance, even if its pursuit involves certain sacrifices. But the main imbalance of the comparison is that while two kinds of experience have been contrasted, only the language of analytical discursive thinking (e.g. in science and technology), with its strengths and necessary limitations, has so far been discussed. But if one is to contrast the *experience* of the uses of discursive language with the concrete experience of flying in a plane or watching one take off, one must also consider the *language*, or languages, in which such personal and particular experiences may be expressed. The language of science and technology is precise and exact, public, conventionally agreed, with its strict rules of usage. As against that (and the attenuated experience it implies) it is not adequate simply to consider concrete experience, very concrete and rich, no doubt, but also in its sensations and feelings very amorphous. If there are precise languages which express abstract thinking, are there, must there not be, 'languages' which express and articulate concrete experiences? Certainly there are, though the word 'languages', set in inverted commas, may be misleading if it is assumed that these other 'languages' are like ordinary public-dictionary-language with its grammar and syntax or the strictly rule-governed languages of science and technology (see Chapter III). But in a wide (or loose) sense of 'language' as expressing and communicating meaning, there are certainly 'languages' which can express and communicate what in the first instance may be personal and private, and very concrete and individual, experience. Further, in the process of expression, embodiment, articulation in a medium, meanings expressed and embodied may take on new significance not known before. The medium, and the media, I have principally but not exclusively in mind here are the media of the arts—all the arts.

The media of the arts are, *par excellence*, media for the expression of concrete human experience. They are not the only media, as I shall discuss later (see Chapters VI and VII). Experiences of *moral* value can be expressed in human character, attitude, action. Relations between ourselves and other *persons* can be expressed in a variety of ways. But the arts historically have always been a central mode of expression of experiences, and of the discovery of new experiences, new meanings, untranslatable back into any other terms or 'language' than their own.

The different media of the several arts have each their own particular potentialities, and limitations, for the expression and discovery of meanings. Literature, prose or poetry, using words, can draw upon, represent and transform ideas and images of all kinds, building them up into new complex imaginative experiences of which we would not have been fully aware but for the artist's versatile and sensitively embodied perceptions. Here is Mary Stewart, conveying the atmosphere of a place, a place in Northumberland, the scene of a burnt-out mansion:

> The woods were quiet and fresh. If they were not full of comfort, at least they offered solitude, and a vast indifference.
>
> I would go on, I thought, a little further; as far as the house. The moonlight was strong, and even when the path turned (as it soon did) away from the river, I could see my way fairly easily.
>
> Presently the timber thinned again, and the path shook itself free of the engulfing rhododendrons, to skirt a knoll where an enormous cedar climbed, layer upon layer, into the night sky. I came abruptly out of the cedar's shadow into a great open space of moonlight, and there at the other side of it, backed against the far wall of trees, was the house.
>
> The clearing where I stood had been a formal garden enclosed by artificial banks where azaleas and berberis grew in a wild tangle. Here and there remains of formal planting could be seen, groups of bushes and small ornamental trees, their roots deep in the rough grass that covered lawns and flower-beds alike . . .
>
> I paused beside the sundial. The scent of the small frilled roses came up thick and sweet, and mixed with honeysuckle. The petals were wet, and the dew was heavy on the grass where I stood.
>
> The shell of the house gaped. Behind it, the high trees made a horizon, against which the moon sketched in the shapes of the broken walls and windows. One end of the house, still roofed and chimneyed, thrust up looking almost intact, till you saw the forest through the window frames.
>
> I crossed the damp, springy grass towards the terrace steps. Somewhere an owl hooted, and a moment later I saw it drift past the blind windows, to be lost in the woods beyond. I hesitated, then slowly climbed the steps. Perhaps it was here that I would find the ghosts . . .[10]

Here the descriptive picture builds up slowly (and this is only a fragment), drawing upon all the senses with an acute 'feel' for their symbolism, metaphor ingredient throughout a contemplative mood. But mood can be expressed sharply, as in W.B. Yeats' 'Never give all the heart':

He that made this knows the cost,
For he gave all his heart and lost.

The sounds of 'cost' and 'lost' seem to epitomize a union of the sharpness of pain and its long durance.

5. Knowledge and understanding

This book is a discussion of different ways or kinds of understanding, different ways, and the forms and structures of different ways, in which personal minds cognitively, through feeling, through activities of various kinds, come to terms with their subject matters in different kinds of situations. There are complex (epistemological) situations in which there is a subject, a personal mind, in cognitive relation to its phenomenal 'objects': i.e. what appears before the mind. The kind of object affects the general mode in which we 'see' things—one mode for mathematics, others for natural or human sciences, philosophy, the arts, theology, religion, with much overlapping and subtle interplay.

'Knowledge' (or cognition) and 'understanding' are distinguishable conceptually, though inseparable existentially, but their emphasis in relation to one another varies. The facts discerned by sense perception are known and taken for granted without usually much need to 'understand' them, except as far as needed for practice. One sees a walking stick, knows what it is, and 'understands' how to use it if necessary. It would seem pedantic to say that one needs to 'understand' it. We 'know' an indefinitely large number of things—geographical, historical, popularly-'scientific'—on authority, often with the most superficial understanding of them. We may 'know' a person, by acquaintance or by reputation, without understanding him or her. We must know a language well enough to be able to understand what is said, or to be able to communicate: but we need not 'know' it or 'understand' it as a linguist does. Generally speaking we have to know enough to understand, and understand enough to know. They are always in some relationship, varying in different cases, but the knowledge and the understanding, as well as their relationship, may be very superficial.

The distinction between knowledge and understanding is not difficult, then, to make at a superficial level. But the distinction at deeper levels, though it still remains as a purely conceptual notion, is very difficult to sustain clearly when one is thinking existentially of the mind at work as a whole. In a scientific or philosophical argument one can still say 'he knows the facts or data, *and* he understands well how to deal with them'. But we would not say, of a great scientist or philosopher, that 'his knowledge is profound' without normally assuming in the statement that his understanding is profound too, and that, in this sort of context, the two are barely distinguishable. It is so because the living mind simply must work, when it is at its best, as a whole. Its 'perspective' is of a world, perhaps of facts, perhaps of value, perhaps of a mixture of both, which is 'seen' (or cognized) in a certain, understanding, perspicacious way.

The human *capacity* for knowing and understanding simply has to be taken for granted, accepted, and cannot be reduced, although of course the ways of its operations have been, and are, subject to endless analysis. Here I shall consider some different ways in which this general thing, which we can only generally label 'understanding', seems to operate in different fields. The fields are, mainly, discursive thinking, intuition, the arts, persons and moral values. It is by looking at this general thing 'understanding' in its concretely different ways of operating, that we can perhaps comprehend a little better the complex yet single mind, *and* its education.

Because, in these various operations *feeling* (as I have already suggested) plays different parts, and because the word is used in many often conflicting ways, it is very necessary first to consider what we mean by 'feeling', and to delineate how the word and concept will be viewed in this book.

Chapter II
Feeling and Thinking

Perhaps nowhere is the divisiveness, the compartmentalization, of thinking, illustrated better than in assumptions about the human mind, that it can be separated into 'faculties' of knowing, thinking, conceptual understanding, on the one hand, and willing and feeling, on the other. In this chapter I shall be concerned more particularly with the division between thinking and feeling, with an allusion here and there to willing.

'Faculty thinking' is supposed to belong to the past and to have been disposed of by now. I imagine that few people would admit to it nowadays. Nevertheless its influence is to be seen in all sorts of ways. It may be 'dead', but it 'won't lie down'. And it is, and was, seen very clearly in the division between thinking and feeling.

Speaking of events at the end of the last century, James Hillman writes (in an article on Jung): 'There were no clear distinctions among the components of the mind which had been grouped, or discarded, in that bag called "the affective faculty". From the time of the Enlightenment in Germany, the soul was divided into three parts: thinking, willing and feeling. Fundamentally, this third region of the psyche, like Plato's third class of men, was inferior.'[1] Furthermore, this bag of feelings was always in opposition to thinking, or, as Moses Mendelssohn said: 'We no longer feel as soon as we think'. Hillman adds that the opposition between thinking and feeling is still found in the scientistic psychology of head without heart, and the romantic psychology of heart without head. This habit of mind is of course much older than the Enlightenment, and newer than the scientism of the earlier part of this century. It goes back to Plato's exaltation of Reason and rational thinking as the exclusive instrument of true knowledge, or, in our own era, to Descartes, the division between rationalism and empiricism, Hume's Reason *or* Sentiment as the foundation of morals ... emotivism in ethics ... the total neglect of feelings in behaviourism. This is an admittedly odd and untidy list. It is meant only to indicate how wide and varied is the habit of separating things which existentially belong together.

1. Earlier theories of feeling

In the psychological literature of the late nineteenth century, and in the twentieth, there has been little satisfactory treatment of feeling. If one looks up the indexes of some of the more or less contemporary books on psychology it is disconcerting to find that the item 'feeling' does not appear. (And this is not confined to books on behaviouristic psychology, where such omission might be expected.) There are voluminous writings on *emotion*—and it is widely assumed, even by the most professional writers, that thinking about emotion is more or less the same thing as thinking about feeling. 'Feeling-and-emotion', 'feeling-or-emotion' are bracketed together as though they were identical. And when it is suggested, say, that action or thinking has a feeling aspect, it is almost a certainty that the psychologist will write 'emotional aspect', and think he or she has been saying the same thing. This is most unfortunate and leads to all sorts of muddles. Feeling, as I shall try to show, is one *aspect* of conscious life, bound up with everything else that happens in conscious life, but still only one aspect of it. Emotion, to quote James Ward, 'is a *complete* state of mind, a psychosis, and not a psychical element, if we may so say'[2] (italic mine). As a gloss on this I may add that the word 'psychosis' was regularly used, in the first two or three decades of the century, to mean, concretely, a total state of the psychophysical organism viewed as living within particular contexts. The word 'psychosis' had nothing to do with the limited meaning imposed on it later by the psychiatrists—of 'psychotic' or 'psychoses'.

Earlier psychologists, like Ward and Stout, who had the great advantage—now mostly missing—of being philosophers before they became psychologists, not only did not confuse feeling with emotion but wrote extensively on both, as distinct fields of investigation. Here I shall be concerned mainly with feeling and not with emotion: I shall therefore now refer briefly to earlier accounts of feeling as a preliminary to a more positive account.

James Ward, in his monumental work *Psychological Principles*, speaks of the wide variation in accounts of feeling in and before his day. Rather understating it, he writes:

Perfect clearness on these points does not seem to exist among psychologists. While it is agreed—practically on all hands—that the ultimate facts of mind are cognition, feeling, and conation, there is no corresponding unanimity either as to the category to which these facts belong or as to how they are related. They are spoken of as processes, states, affections, action, and so on: formerly they were for the most part dealt with in separation as the 'energies' or 'functions' of corresponding faculties. At other times we are told that 'they are never presented to us separately, but always in conjunction and that it is only by an ideal analysis that they can be discriminated and considered apart'. But feeling and cognition are sometimes represented as antithetical, 'in inverse ratio'; sometimes it is said feeling may be absent altogether: by some, 'will' is said to be dependent throughout on feeling, by others it is regarded as a veritable *primum movens*.

And when we come to feeling itself, Ward writes of 'the doctrine that feeling alone is primordial and invariably present wherever there is consciousness at all', that this doctrine derives its plausibility partly from the vagueness of the word 'feeling',

and partly from the intimate connexion that undoubtedly exists between feeling and cognition on the one hand and feeling and volition on the other. As to the meaning of the term, it is plain that further definition is requisite for a word that may denote (a) a touch, as feeling of roughness; (b) an organic sensation, as feeling of hunger; (c) an emotion, as feeling of anger; (d) *any* purely subjective state, as feeling of certainty or of activity; (e) the *one* subjective state that is purely 'affective', as feeling of pleasure or pain.[3]

And he adds that we find the same variety of usage in the German *Gefühl* and the French *sentiment*. Endeavouring to find a common characteristic in all of these meanings, he settles on 'the feeling of pleasure or pain'. This, or 'hedonic tone' (positive or negative), was indeed the generally accepted meaning of 'feeling' in those days—and has been to a considerable extent since. Stout[4] holds the same view. Such a view, however, seems to me to be quite inadequate, much too limiting. Ward's method of attempting to abstract a common element from the various uses of the word, gives to 'feeling' the most attenuated character, and does no justice to the important part which feeling plays throughout the whole of conscious life. Some degree of 'pleasure' or 'pain' (physical or mental) may indeed characterize a great deal—not necessarily all—of conscious life. But this is a highly abstract statement, and refers to one single aspect of experience picked out from it in all its concreteness. It seems to me that here we need what used to be called a 'concrete universal', not an abstract one. Pleasure–pain, hedonic tone, in itself tells us the very minimum about feeling. It is the thinnest possible of concepts. Instead of accepting that, I think that we should look at how the thing we call 'feeling' operates in our concrete experience. I shall, in the main body of the book, try to show how feeling operates in various fields of experience—the arts, the knowledge and understanding of persons, moral values, and conceptual thinking itself.

Ward, in the passage quoted above, refers to 'the doctrine that feeling alone is primordial and invariably present wherever there is consciousness at all'. Susanne Langer in her book, *Mind: an Essay on Human Feeling* (one of the rare examples of systematic treatment of the subject), takes up the same theme. Feeling is indefinable, except by so-called 'ostensive' definition: but it can be *displayed* in examples of its different manifestations. According to Langer, feeling, 'the mark of mentality', emerges at a certain stage of evolution when a 'neurophysiological process can be said to "break through to feeling" '.[5]

> [The] phenomenon usually described as 'a feeling' is really that an organism feels something, i.e. something is felt. What is felt is a process, perhaps a large complex of processes, within the organism. Some vital activities of great complexity and high intensity, usually (perhaps always) involving nervous tissue, are felt; being felt is a phase of the process itself. A phase is a mode of appearance, and not an added factor . . . When iron is heated to a critical degree it becomes red; yet its redness is not a new entity which must have gone somewhere else when it is no longer in the iron. It was a phase of the iron itself, at high temperature.[6]

Like—analogously—the incandescence of a piece of iron at a high temperature, feeling is living process becoming aware of itself.

At this primitive stage feeling just seems to happen, and this consciousness, the emergence of the primitively psychological from the irritable physiological, is a mystery no one yet has begun to understand. But two things have to be kept in mind: (1) the *inseparability* of organic processes from the organism's feeling of it, the fact that, as Langer puts it, the 'being felt is a phase of the process itself'; on the other hand (2) there is the *conceptual distinction* between the feeling which is (if primitively) mental, and the organic processes which are felt.

These speculations may or may not be found helpful as an approach to the better understanding of the function of feeling in the organization and economy of the human psychophysical organism. It is to an attempt towards this better understanding that I now turn. And, as the earlier accounts of feeling as hedonic tone, pleasure–pain, or as purely 'affective', seem to me to be totally inadequate, and little clear writing has emerged since, I shall have to start afresh. For me it is certainly not a new start, for I have been toying with the idea of feeling as an integral part of knowing and understanding in books and papers since the 1920s.[7] But what follows must stand for itself.

(Perhaps I ought to say here that although I have referred mostly to the narrow view of feeling, I know that the word 'feeling' is often used in a wider sense, and particularly as if it were cognitive. We all at times speak of cognitive 'feelings' about moral and humanitarian matters, about people, works of art, political decisions. Ryle listed different uses of the word 'feeling', some of which are cognitive-claiming. Jung uses 'feeling' in various cognitive ways, but very pragmatically and often inconsistently. 'Feeling' is used cognitively by philosophers—existentialists, phenomenologists . . . by James, Bradley, Alexander, Whitehead, Mac-Murray . . . by Gestalt psychologists—in a large variety of ways. And the linking of *emotion* with the cognitive—clearly understood by Ward and Stout—was, as it were, rediscovered in the 1950s by Bedford, J.R. Jones, Kenny, Peters, Mace. I am all for a wider use: but I think a reassessment of what 'feeling' is is necessary in order to justify this wider use.)

2. A positive account of feeling

My very general theme is that feeling is an inseparable part of everything that happens in the conscious life of the psychophysical organism. One of the most important aspects of this is the relation of feeling to cognition.

Feeling, on one side of it, is the most immediate, the most private, the most intimate thing we know. 'I feel; I feel, alone; alone, I feel'; no one else can know my 'I feel'. And if I feel, I feel *something*. Langer says that feeling is living process becoming aware of itself. If we apply this to the 'living process' of human beings, feeling will be a process of human life becoming aware of itself, or as aware of itself. And as it is human life—and not merely 'living process' as one might apply the term to a lower organism—feeling will be, potentially, immediate awareness of the whole content of human experience as it is lived by a human being. Feeling is the immediate awareness, from the 'inside', of conscious human experience in the widest and most usually accepted sense of that term, conscious experience which in human beings includes bodily sensations, actions of various kinds, thinking, imagining, willing, having moral and aesthetic experiences, perhaps religious ones, loving, hating, coming to know and coming to terms with the external world, ourselves and other people. Feeling is the immediate awareness of indwelling in that conscious life in its most inclusive sense. To symbolize the conceptual distinction between feeling—the participle, being immediately aware—and its content, I shall sometimes use 'IA' to stand for the participles denoting the process or event of feeling or immediate awareness, and 'C' for the content of feeling. Feeling as it actually occurs is always IA(C).

Feeling is present throughout conscious life. But caution is needed here. This does not mean that we are focally conscious of it all the time. Usually we are not. Sometimes it is marginal, and sometimes it *seems* to be absent altogether—lacing one's shoes, for example. Though we can be aware of feeling ourselves inhabiting our bodies, for the most part there is no such conscious awareness.

I am, then, *not* saying that we always feel ourselves feeling, are immediately aware of ourselves as immediately aware, or feel *that* we are feeling or being immediately aware.* Sometimes we can be: and *afterwards* in retrospection we may be able to discern the presence of the factor of feeling of which we were perhaps not at all conscious at the time.

In the normal situation attention is not turned inwards but outwards. If, for instance, we engage in or are attending to an interesting argument, or listening to a piece of fine music, our attention is completely absorbed in what is being attended to, the argument or the music. The object of attention completely fills up the field. But though this is certainly true, and very important, retrospection, which we can carry out as self-conscious human beings, does not bear out any impression that there was no feeling present at the time. There was cognitive feeling, the 'feeling through' of the argument, the 'feeling through' of the structured music. And there was affect. The argument was perhaps exciting, and we enjoyed it. In the objective, holistic absorption in the music, there was enjoyment, perhaps raptured enjoyment.

But situations vary. If suddenly we witness a terrible street accident, we do not just 'witness' it; we are at the same time transfixed by horror, and certainly aware of a feeling of horror. And in some cases, according to temperament, we turn away from it, sick with horror—particularly if

---

* Diagrammatically, in terms of the symbols used, this could be formally stated as (a) IA(C), where (C) would be IA(C) itself, and (b) as IA(C) where (C) would be *that* we are feeling *that* there is IA(C). Usually, as I am going on to say, the content of feeling (C) is other than IA(C). The content, or object, (C) of feeling is *what* we are attending to, and not feeling itself.

we can do nothing about it. Speaking generally, we cannot eliminate the truth that in enjoyable intellectual or aesthetic experiences, we feel, in those cases, both cognitively and affectively. Completely absorbed by the fascination of the argument or the delight in the music we may not be aware of it even as enjoyment. But it is there all the same. In the case of the accident feeling (here emotional) is markedly present.

Here, it will be noticed, I am distinguishing feeling (IA(C)) from *affect*. This is important, for in common psychological parlance 'feeling' and 'affect' are used indiscriminately as meaning the same thing. And because, as we have seen, the word 'affect' is used commonly to denote hedonic tone, positive or negative, the identification of feeling simply with affect could take us back to the view I have rejected, that feeling just *is* pleasure–pain. But feeling is not to be identified with affect, though it can *have* affect. And I am repeating that if so, the affect which feeling may have is not adequately described as hedonic tone, pleasure–pain— though the terms pleasure and pain do have some use as rough indicators. We all recognize what they mean. But they are far too general to give any idea of the unlimited range of the *concrete* qualities of affect. We have to remember that feeling (IA(C)) is cognitive. If, as I have suggested, feeling is the immediate awareness 'from the inside' of all that goes on in conscious human experience, then the affect of feeling, inseparable from it, is as wide in concrete content as the range of human experience itself. To repeat, feeling is not, qua immediate awareness, identical with affect. Feeling is immediate awareness of human experience from the inside, and as such cognitive. As this, it *has* affect sometimes. So, generalizing, feeling has (at least) two distinguishable aspects, the cognitive and the affective. If sometimes I speak of 'affective feeling' and 'cognitive feeling', this has to be understood as shorthand for feeling in its affective or in its cognitive aspect.

It is because feeling or immediate awareness is potentially feeling of everything that goes on in conscious experience that the content and particular quality of affect is unlimited in its range. And since the range of our language is limited, by practical or theoretical interests, there are no names for the contents of most of our great range of feelings. For a few common emotions, moods, feelings, we have names—anger, sex, fear ... weary, depressed, anxious, joyous ... hungry, stomach ache, physically energetic ... mentally energetic, 'flat', puzzled ... But for most of our feelings there are no names at all. They are real enough, but they overlap and are indefinitely complex. Much may be expressed in subtle nuances of behaviour—tones of voice, gesture. And of course they may be sensitively described at length by literary artists. But in potentially infinitely varying circumstances there is infinitely varying cognitive and affective content, and therefore infinitely various concrete feelings.

There may seem to be a contradiction here. The account of feeling I have given so far is an account of it as, in a sense, cognitive, the sense in which immediate awareness of content can be called 'cognitive'. But if, as has just been suggested, a large part of the content of feeling cannot be named or categorized, are we justified in calling the awareness which is feeling 'cognitive'? Clearly it cannot be so if the current and conventional view is being assumed, that the range of cognition is properly confined to what can be clearly categorized in concepts which can be articulated in words or other symbols, and expressed in propositional form. But, as I have already indicated, this is not being assumed here. Feeling (IA) is cognitive in always having content (C): in feeling we must always feel *something*, though for the most part we do not 'know' *what* we feel. And, speaking generally, there is a wide range of knowledge in which feeling is involved, which cannot be categorized or expressed in propositional form. There is direct knowledge of people, of art, of moral values . . . and, as I shall try to show in this book, none of it can be adequately expressed in words or stated in general propositional language.

I distinguish, then, two senses in which feeling is related to the cognitive. As immediate awareness of content, feeling is, in the usage I am adopting, cognitive in its own right, whether or not there is any language with which to categorize it conceptually. Where there is such language, there may still be a limiting case in which we can be said to be cognitively aware of a content (i.e. to feel) without conceptual categorization. If I receive a sudden blow from behind, I may definitely feel 'something' before I have even time to flash the question, 'What's that?' Or for a fraction of time when coming out from being under an anaesthetic, I may feel an inchoate mass of pain (that is, of what I am *now* calling 'pain') without realizing *what* it is. But after this fraction of time, when I can think, 'Someone's hit me' or 'I've just had an operation', the cognition comes into a different category, the familiar one of knowing-that, or knowing-what. I am saying that immediate awareness of content without a concept, or marginally without awareness of a concept, is one form of cognition. The familiar case of cognizing under a concept is another.

Since this is all very complex, I had better try to sum it up in different words. Feeling or immediate awareness is something which is not definable further: it is one of the evident but mysterious facts of nature. In human beings it ranges downwards from first infantile consciousness, and upwards to highest human experience. We suppose it present in animals, but we can only postulate this and by speculative extrapolation dimly imagine. In animals and infants it may be called 'pre-reflective' in a phylogenetic sense: in these early stages reflection, as we use the term of a power of mature human beings, is simply not possible. But there is sometimes a 'pre-reflective' stage in another, ontogenetic, sense: the example of waking up from an anaesthetic would apply here. There can be an instant or short period *before* we reflect. We are immediately aware, perhaps, of an inchoate mass of sensationally painful *something*. It is not, at that moment, even some 'thing', for at that moment, as pre-reflective, it is linguistically preconceptual. The instant we recover full consciousness it will go, 'pop', into a linguistic category. I remember, long ago, falling off a bus on to my head. I felt, or heard, what I can only call (now) a sort of vibratory noise. There was a distinct pause. Then: 'That was my head!' In both phylogenetic and ontogenetic pre-reflective feeling, then, there is content, but unspecifiable, or as yet unspecified.

In the ordinary course of conscious life, feeling has, as I have been repeatedly saying, potentially a very wide range of possible content. A chief distinction is between sensational content and mental content. One can be immediately aware of, or feel, bodily sensations, massively organic, or of the special senses. Or one can be aware of oneself as thinking and imagining. But of course *what* one is immediately aware of at any one time will depend on what is in the foreground of consciousness at that time. I feel, potentially indwell, within the whole of my experience, but the particular quality and character of my feeling at any one time will depend on what is being attended to, or what is of interest, at that particular time. The qualities of feeling are as wide ranging as the range of experience itself. As for affect, it may be positively hedonically toned, or negatively toned, or it may be more or less 'neutral'.

The question of the relation of feeling to cognition and to conation is complex. The question depends in part on whether one is thinking of cognition in the sense in which it can be expressed in propositional statements, or in other senses, mentioned above, of knowing in fields such as the arts, the knowing of persons or of moral values. These latter senses I shall be considering more fully in other chapters of the book. Now let us look at the relation of feeling as it has been described, to cognition and conation, with a main emphasis on propositional knowledge-that.

3. Cognition, conation, and feeling: the cognitive contents of feeling

I am assuming that cognition, conation and feeling are inseparable aspects or facets of conscious life. If we use the word 'faculty'—harmless enough in itself—it must never be thought to imply watertight compartments. It is difficult to find language here to express at the same time *distinctions* of nature and function, with the other side of the picture, that cognition, conation and feeling are *always* present, always together, always functioning in co-operation, and in indefinitely various situations which are so particular and so complex that to try to state the organically dynamic form of the structure and functions would be an endless task. All I can do is to suggest in a few broad and general statements the complexity and the unity of it all.

We cannot *think* without conative activity, without some interest in what we are thinking about. We cannot actively conate without some object or objects in mind, perhaps vague, but often at least potentially thinkable under concepts. This is a conventional and cautious statement and, in implication, very complex. If the situation is one in which we are trying to think intellectually, as in mathematics, science or philosophy, the focus will be on at least what is potentially stateable in propositions using the appropriate symbols of these enquiries, and it is presupposed that such statements will illuminate our understanding of their subject matters. If the conational striving is focused on some proposed practical enterprise, again this enterprise will be apprehended partly in terms of concepts. If the enterprise is in the field of the arts, whether it is the enterprise of the creative artist, or of the spectator of art trying to understand it discriminatingly, the conative object will still, but only up to a point, be thinkable conceptually. An artist in the throes of making has *some* idea of what he/she wants to express through its embodiment in a medium, and the idea could, in the earlier stages of the making, perhaps be vaguely stated in words. However, even if the artist happens to be a poet who uses words, it is in the nature of art that he/she does not fully know what the idea is before starting. Moreover, when he/she has 'finished', the idea is not something which can ever be said adequately in terms other than those in which his/her art presents it to us. If it is a poem, there can never be an adequate paraphrase of it. The same holds for other arts. The discriminating spectator of given art, on the other hand, can talk—either as a 'second-order' critic or as a 'third-order' philosopher of aesthetics—sensibly *about* the art or arts. But such talk, in ordinary conceptual language, is illuminating only in so far as it helps us towards the special kind of understanding which is aesthetic, and which cannot be said in words. (On this, see Chapters IV and V.)

Again, if feeling or immediate awareness is present throughout waking life, it follows that we cannot think or conate without feeling. If we are thinking intellectually, there is underlying immediate awareness of our thinking. This does not mean, as I have said, that we are focally or self-consciously aware of our awareness, noticing it, focusing on it, except when we are performing an (unnatural) introspection. If we are thinking intellectually about some problem, the focus of attention is on the problem and the feeling of thinking about it, tacit or subsidiary. And in a case like this there may be very little marked affect. Since we are to some degree interested in what we are thinking about, there will probably be some affect, the positive or negative tone of which will to some extent depend on whether the thinking is going well or badly. If positive, the vigour of the thinking tends to be reinforced, if negative, to be inhibited. Affective feeling can then be an auxiliary of intellectual thinking. But affective feeling is not relevant to the end result, which is, I am assuming, clear, objective, impersonal statement of facts or concepts, statement which does not relevantly reveal the thinker's affective feelings.

But the way in which feeling functions, and the extent to which it is relevant or irrelevant to the end result, will (again) depend on the kind of object which is before consciousness, the sort of interest we have in it, and whether affect is intrinsic, internally related to the knowledge and understanding of the object before us. As we have just seen, if the interest is merely in the clear literal statement of facts or concepts, the thinker's affect is not relevant to the end result. If, on the other hand, the object before consciousness is now important because it involves considerations of *value*, the situation is different. If the object is aesthetic, or the question is one of moral good or evil, and our interest is in *that*, the factor of cognitive-and-affective feeling will—as I shall try to show in some detail later—be very relevant indeed. Feeling, and some awareness of it as affective, will be marginally, and at times focally, present; and it will be important in the final determination of the aesthetic or moral judgement. I hope to show that the apprehension of neither aesthetic nor moral values is possible without feeling, with the cognitive and affective indivisibly united and fused together. One cannot appreciate a beautiful shell, or work of art, or a morally compassionate action, except in a total apprehension in which cognition, conation and feeling are working together as one.

In all this, though, it is sometimes convenient to speak of 'cognitive feeling', or perhaps 'conative thinking'. It must be stressed that these are only shorthand expressions of an emphasis. It is not 'cognition' that knows, 'conation' that strives, or 'feeling' that feels. It is the whole person, the human psychophysical organism, who apprehends through these modes of itself.

I began by saying that feeling, on one side of it 'is the most immediate, the most private, the most intimate thing we know'. But in considering the varieties of the content of feeling, it should now be clear that although *some* of the content of feeling is of subjective states, bodily and mental, this is only one area of the content of feeling. Feeling is 'indwelling' in conscious life 'in its most inclusive sense', of which the content of introspective feeling is only one factor; and introspection, as we know, is in some ways an artificial and inadequate process. The psychophysical organism lives in a world external to itself, in which, as mind, it is interested in all kinds of ways, cognitively, practically and feelingly. And feeling, as immediate experience, shares in the cognitiveness, the practical responses, the qualities of these in their outward-directed activities, activities which, as outwardly directed, are transitive or self-transcending. Nearly sixty years ago I suggested some of the implications of this in several papers.[8] I would not want now to express in the same way everything that was said there; but one main contention I still think true: that feeling does share in the objectively directed character of our cognitive–conative relations with the world. We feel the whole transitive cognitive–conative process, outwardly directed towards the world. In this sense feeling is not only cognitive of immediate physical–mental content; as sharing with and being organic with cognition and conation it is also cognitive of *objects* in the world.

For convenience sake we may distinguish between *contents* of cognition, a widely inclusive category, and *objects* of cognition, a narrower one. One range of *contents* I have already specified—those, physical and mental, which belong to our private worlds. Of these contents of immediate experience or feeling, some can be specified and, as I suggested, have familiar names—physical pains like toothache or stomach ache or a sense of physical wellbeing . . . or anxiety, fear, aggressiveness, sex . . . These, having names, names of familiar experienced states, can be subsumed under concepts. They are states which can be subsumed under class-concepts, and are *contents* which are also *objects*. There are, as we noted, many others, elusive, complex and indescribable, known directly in their individual qualities, but which, because individual and particular, and having no names, fall into no neat categories. And what is true here is also true of cognitive contents which pertain to the external independent world. For common sense, science and philosophy, there are many contents of cognition which are clearly specifiable under concepts—chairs, tables, trees . . . gravitational equations, substances, qualities, relations, protons, electrons . . . physical, mental, facts, values . . . Others, more particular and individual—aesthetic qualities we experience in nature or in works of art; or of individual persons, or of specific personal moral actions—are specifiable only up to a point, and beyond that, no. There are some general aesthetic words—gay, delicate, profound, beautiful, ugly . . . There are general categories of art, schools and movements in art—post-impressionist, cubist, abstract-impressionist, classical, romantic, realistic . . . There are general words too in speaking of personal qualities or of moral values. But as I shall try to emphasize, all these, which come under the general heading of value judgements (or if they are descriptive words, related to value judgements) manifest their full concrete meaning only in particulars and individuals. One has to go and look . . . listen . . . They can be intuitively known in all their individuality: but they cannot properly be described in words. I am not, in all this, trying to divide thinking in terms of concepts from the intuitions of particulars and individuals, particularly in the field of values. As language-using, all our thinking is charged with the influence of conceptual propositional language: and our conceptual thinking is not separate from feeling. But emphases are different. Some forms of conceptual thinking, though motivated by cognitive–conative feeling, are, in the actual processes of their working, relatively free from conscious feeling. T.H. Huxley spoke of the 'clear cold logic of the mind'. Their products likewise are judged with cool objectivity. In the arts, as I shall show, objectivity of judgement is of great importance. But in making art, and in the appreciation and criticism of made art, feeling plays a prominent part—though it is indivisibly a thinking process too. But always it is the whole person at work.

Chapter III
Kinds of Knowing

1. Acquaintance: intuition and thinking

The broad distinction made by Bertrand Russell in his *Problems of Philosophy*,[1] between knowledge by acquaintance and knowledge by description, is a fundamental one. Acquaintance-knowledge, as I shall take it here, is direct knowledge of particulars or individuals, not—for reasons which will appear—of abstract concepts or universals as such. One may describe particulars or individuals, in the sense of describing seriatim their features. The description uses general words: this is a 'long' 'red' 'pencil' with a 'fibre' 'point'. The general words stand for abstracted concepts. In contrast, the pencil as directly perceived, possesses its qualities in inseparable relations to one another, concretely not abstractly. In hearing descriptions, particularly of familiar objects like pencils, this difference is not noticed, because the description is of a familiar thing which can instantly be imagined, 'seen in the mind's eye', and 'seen' concretely as in direct perception. But strictly speaking no description ever adds up to acquaintance-knowledge, as is seen much more clearly when the thing described is not a familiar object but, say, an unknown person or work of art. This is not, however, to say that the use of description cannot, retroactively, enhance and enrich the perceived content of what is directly apprehended.

In respect of its directness, acquaintance-knowledge may be called intuitive. But the range of the content of 'intuition', as I shall use the word, is much wider than the range of acquaintance, in fact is as wide as the range of knowledge itself. As well as having intuitions of particular and individual things, we can intuit abstract concepts, universals—axioms, the laws of thought, conceptual relations, systems of ideas.

But the word 'intuition' is very much misunderstood, and very much abused. It is abused by ordinary people who want to avoid thinking, by philosophers who without much examination dismiss it as mere subjective hunch opposed to reason. R.S. Peters couples 'wild and intuitive'.[2] Intuition in ethics is often assumed to be necessarily exclusive of reasoned judgement; and if art is said to be understood intuitively, this is supposed to be the functioning of an isolated faculty cut off from rational discussion. Because of all this, it is necessary to consider carefully the meaning and application of 'intuition', and its presence as a crucial factor in all knowledge whatsoever. The limitations expressed in this paragraph are I think absurd and could be called scandalous! There can be no knowledge of any subject—mathematics, any science or art, philosophy, history—or any value without at many stages direct intuitive grasp of the subject matter, parts in relation to wholes.

A.R. Lacey in his *Dictionary of Philosophy*[3] says of intuition: 'generally a direct relation between the mind and some object, analogous to what common sense thinks is the relation between us and something we see unambiguously in a clear light'. He adds: 'The emphasis is on the directness of the relation . . .' The *Concise Oxford Dictionary* version is: 'Immediate apprehension by the mind without reasoning; immediate apprehension by sense; immediate insight'.

Lacey's emphasis on directness of relation between the mind and an object (we may add 'as a whole') is acceptable. But, being hypercritical, we might question 'in a clear light'. For some intuitions can be vague, foggy, obscure. So too the Oxford Dictionary's 'immediate insight' may be questioned. Intuitions can conceal misconceptions or totally erroneous assumptions. Again, the Dictionary's 'without reasoning', though a fair description which may be accepted in the sense in which it is meant, must be taken with caution. If the emphasis is on reason*ing*, the description is broadly true. But in the case of mathematical axioms, or the 'laws' of thought (e.g. identity, non-contradiction), usually regarded as intuitively accepted, is the most self-evident immediate reasoning entirely absent? And in some intuitions there may be reasoning so rapid that we are unaware of it; or there may be workings of the subconscious mind, individual or collective, as well as the mass of tacit knowledge (including past reasonings) which is always there. Though the absence of explicit reasoning is certainly a general character of intuition, we ought not to assume that intuition is thereby cut off from reasoned thinking.

A general distinction can sometimes be made between intuitions which are at the basis of certain processes of thinking and are presupposed in it, and intuitions which clearly supervene upon a process of thinking, which presuppose a process of thinking. For convenience I shall call them 'primary' and 'secondary' intuitions. Axioms and laws of thought would be examples of primary intuitions. Synoptic intuitions which one can have on viewing in retrospect and seeing a piece of discursive reasoning immediately as a whole, would be examples of secondary intuitions.

The term 'primary' can most clearly be applied to mathematical or logical systems based upon postulates and axioms—in Euclid, for instance. In a very different sense the laws of logical thought are primary in relation to discursive arguments, though the explicit formulation of them does not have to be made before thinking begins: people could think logically before Aristotle formulated the laws. But in fields other than purely logical ones the distinction between primary and secondary intuitions is not nearly so clear-cut, and has to be used pragmatically as far as it is relevant and useful. It is difficult to be sure, for instance, whether there are any truly primary intuitions in moral or aesthetic fields, or if there are, in what sense and where they occur. Some moralists make intuitions of right primary: I prefer to say intuitions of good are primary—though this certainly allows intuitions of right too (see Chapter VII). But whether there are such intuitions, or what they are 'of', is a matter for argument. And it could be contended, for instance, that if there are moral 'intuitions' at all they are the product of sophisticated thinking and experience—and so really secondary and not primary. I shall return to this kind of question in discussing aesthetic and moral intuitions.

Let us look now at the development and functioning of secondary intuitions in some instances of concrete thinking—'concrete' with an etymological emphasis, with a suggestion of thinking in which ideas 'grow together'. There is a sense in which in any piece of mental understanding, ideas 'grow together'. I have here, however, particularly in mind the kind of concrete thinking—as in philosophy, in theoretical and practical moral thinking and planning and, perhaps, in a rather different sense, in aesthetic thinking about art or the making and appreciating of it—where knowledge and understanding are a growth to clearer, more coherent, more illuminated intuitions. The *process* of philosophical thinking is not like its successful *product*, say, a clearly set out philosophical thesis. It is a struggle of the personal mind, often a struggle in the dark to overcome confusion. If it is succeeding (and how often it does not succeed!), then ideas which earlier seemed remote or obscure can become relevant and illuminating; a new and more coherent perspective comes into view: in the later stages of thought what had seemed disparate elements now appear to have found their proper place in a more coherent and comprehensive whole, which is the content of this later intuition. The same kind of thing can happen as *moral* experience and thinking mature; insight and sometimes moral wisdom both in moral thinking and in moral practice develop, so that the moral agent sees and acts with intuitive insight where earlier he/she may have been baffled and confused. So it is too with ordinary practical thinking and planning. A plan, now seen as a clear and coherent whole, emerges perhaps from obscurity and muddle. If this is true, it shows that it is important to make some such distinction as that between primary and secondary intuitions, the secondary, synoptic perspectives changing and growing with changing and growing thought. These secondary intuitions have a far more important part to play in the life of thinking and doing than is sometimes realized. Intuitions tend to be suspect because they are supposed to be rigid and irrational. 'I just *know*.' But there is nothing in the concept of intuitions which makes them either rigid or irrational. The experienced teacher in the classroom uses his/her intuition every hour of the day. It is the student-teacher who is worried by the search for explicit reasons.

It should be clear from what has been said that intuitions by themselves carry no guarantee of validity, also that they are not, as such, merely subjective. They can be subjective, as when someone says 'I just *know*', where the expression is merely of a groundless but compelling belief. It is unfortunate that, even among otherwise serious thinkers the popular notion that this is just what intuition is, is taken over uncritically. As I mentioned, R.S. Peters couples—rather sweepingly—'wild and intuitive'; and this is not an uncommon way of dismissing intuition offhand. (I am not denying that there can be 'wild' intuitions!)⋆

So far I have been thinking of intuition in relation to mainly intellec-

---

⋆ Intuition is not merely dismissed. It is sometimes (following the popular usage I have just mentioned) positively affirmed to be subjective. David Best, for instance, in 'The objectivity of artistic appreciation', *British Journal of Aesthetics* (Spring 1980, p. 117), defines 'subjective' from the Oxford Dictionary as 'belonging to the perceiving subject, i.e., to personal idiosyncrasy or purely private experience, as opposed to the objective, which depends on real or external things', and cites me as an aesthetic subjectivist. This is, he says, because I 'resort to intuition'. (He also calls me a subjectivist because I say that feelings 'analytically and abstractly regarded'—that is, in certain respects—'belong to the side of the subject and not of the object'.) But no inference to subjectivism can be drawn here. Of course there is a subjective side to intuiting and intuition, as there is in all cognitive processes whatever: it is subjects who do the thinking—a mental process which on one side of it is private. But that this use of intuition implies 'subjectivism', I categorically deny.

tual analytic-synthetic thinking, with mention here and there of its operation in matters of value, moral or aesthetic. These I shall be considering specially in later chapters. But the problems of understanding and conceptual thinking are so different in matters of moral and artistic value (as well as when the understanding of other persons is in question), that it is necessary now to make some preliminary and preparatory observations which bear upon them—and particularly on the knowledge and understanding of art.

2. Intuition, propositional thinking, and art

When we talk about art in general terms or about particular works, we necessarily use conceptual terms. We speak of the 'visual arts', or 'painting', 'sculpture', 'etching', 'silk screen printing'; we speak of music as 'symphonic', 'operatic', 'chamber', 'choral', and so on; or of 'poetry', or 'the novel'. In referring to particular works, we may say of a Cézanne or a Van Gogh that it depicts a human figure or a landscape and that in each of them there are infinitely numerous characteristics and interrelationships. All the special words mentioned are general or abstract; and ordinary speech is always like this.

But although all that can be taken for granted, it is not as though they were 'described' concepts that we approach works of art. It is as individuals that we approach them, and directly, intuitively. And a major question for us in this book is, can we properly be said to *know* individuals—particular works of art, particular persons, the moral value of particular characters or actions? About some general problems of the possibility of 'knowing' art—which is a most difficult puzzle—I shall have some preliminary things to say now, reserving main treatment of the several themes for other chapters.

Since the prevailing and dominant view of what knowledge is is that it is sufficiently grounded in factual-perceptual and/or conceptual evidence, and since claimed 'knowledge' of art does not appear to fit into this pattern without impossible strains, the conclusion would seem to be either that the experience of art is not knowledge but maybe a kind of feeling or emotion, or that if knowledge, that knowledge must be *sui generis*. I shall argue for the latter alternative. But since for most of this century aesthetics has been, at least in these islands, an off-beat and scarcely respectable branch of philosophy, and since the epistemology of art is so dauntingly difficult, the lay philosopher sympathetic to the arts has tended to settle down to the comfortable view that the arts are chiefly to be valued for the pleasure and emotional satisfaction that they yield. That they can give such pleasure and satisfaction and that this is a vitally important aspect of the experience of them, nobody will want to deny. But in the experience of the arts do we not, minds and bodies together, psychophysical organisms working as a whole, also enter directly upon insights unknown to intellect functioning in its relative isolation?

> Reason has moons, but moons not hers,
> Lie mirrored on her sea,
> Confounding her astronomers,
> But, O! delighting me.
> (Ralph Hodgson, 1871–1962)

An obstacle—I think an insuperable obstacle—to the recognition that experience of the arts can be a form of knowledge, is this current, generally accepted and assumed view of knowledge (described in Chapter I) as dependent on propositional truth. Knowledge is tightly tied in with propositional truth. And a proposition is 'true' when it states a fact or—but with some technical reservations—when it 'corresponds' with a fact. Although there may be recognition of 'knowledge by acquaintance' this is not thought to be really and truly knowledge until it has been reduced to some form of propositional knowledge-that. I believe that the limitations of this position are its fatal flaw, and that the assumption of it dogmatically bars the way to the acceptance and understanding of knowledge which is other than discursive. This we have seen is not a minor matter but something which affects our whole culture, and its ideas of what is worth learning in education. It is indispensably important to have knowledge of facts of all kinds and to have, and increase, intellectual understanding of the world. But our beliefs, our beliefs in *values*, what of them? Knowledge of 'what is the case' is not a sufficient basis for knowledge of what ought to be in human relationships or of what is precious in the treasures of the arts. There are beliefs, and there is knowledge which are of the utmost personal importance to human beings in their ordinary—or extraordinary—everyday lives. Can we not validate it in experience, without reducing it to argument or proposition-making?

In the conventional propositional definition of knowledge, the word 'believe' does occur. But the 'belief' assumed is often an attenuated, thinned-down affair, the emphasis of which is entirely on its object, 'that-P'. It is mostly a purely intellectual, abstract cognitive projection, cut off from the rest of active feeling mind. It is not in the least comparable with belief one might have in a religious or moral value, or in a cause or person. The belief can be a sort of raw grunt that '*X* is the case'. It can be purged of all feeling and will—as far as this is possible. (Compare 'We no longer feel as soon as we think'.) On relatively trifling matters this is of no account, but it does no justice to the complex personal factors which inter-penetrate a great deal of our thinking and knowledge-seeking—in, for example, notable scientific discoveries. The older idealists were wiser when they made *judgements* (by the person), rather than propositions, the centre of their epistemological logic.

If knowing and knowledge are always, on one side, a personal matter, something—whether an apprehension of some trifling fact, or of some matter of moment—cognitively possessed by a person, this side is something which ought to be given a positive place in any account of the *truth* of knowledge. If I know, and understand what I know, expressing it (in some kinds of knowledge) in a propositional statement, it is I, personally, who can be said to have, in a common phrase, cognitively 'grasped' it. It is I who 'possess' it.

This is one side. The other side is, of course, its 'public' objectivity and truth, its 'what is the case'. We say, 'He/she has grasped truly, and with understanding, the facts'. In knowledge expressed propositionally, his/her statement is said—in popular usage—to 'correspond' with the facts.

In this propositional account, practically all the emphasis is on the clarity of the propositional statement, and the truth of the *statement*. It looks as if the propositional statement almost stood by itself, with total impersonality, an independent entity. But of course we also know that the statements are made by personal minds and are understood by minds and would be meaningless unless this were so. So, though it looks sometimes as though the necessary and sufficient condition of truth were its impersonal relation to fact, this is not so. It is possible to say that fact is just fact independently of mind; but 'truth' is a meaningless term except in its relation to living mind. If there is truth, there has to be *judgement* of truth; and the propositional statement is the linguistic expression of knowing, understanding mind, cognizing mind in relation to its objects. The conventional view of knowledge of fact, I am saying, though it does mention belief, and grounds for belief, tends to do less than justice, in its stress on the unquestionably impersonal side of knowledge, to the way in which the personal mind is involved, and potentially can be involved, in its many kinds of adventures of knowing and living. And I want now to suggest a view of knowledge which positively asserts that the truth of true knowledge is not ultimately the conformity of statement with fact—which is impersonal and formal, and exclusive to the knowledge which can be expressed in linguistic statements—but the *adequacy* of the cognitive grasp of its objects by personal living mind. The complexity of the nature of this adequacy, and the complexity of its demands upon the resources of the whole person who is struggling after it, varies very much. But it is exemplified in the adventures of scientific discovery, or in the creating and in the understanding of great art.

3. Truth as efficiency of cognitive mind; implications for value-knowledge

What immediately follows has its roots in a book I wrote which was published in 1923, *Knowledge and Truth—an Epistemological Study.*[4] This work dealt with theories of knowledge and truth then current—the Coherence view, American New Realism, Samuel Alexander, Russell's two theories of Correspondence, Critical Realism. It concluded with a chapter on 'Non-propositional truth' (with some reference to the arts) preceded by the suggestion of an independent theory, to which I shall now very briefly refer. (Wittgenstein's correspondence view, of the *Tractatus*, appeared less than a year before mine: I had not then read it.)

Two main factors were criticized. One was general, that knowledge is defined in terms of propositional statements. The other was particular, that knowledge was defined in terms of the justifiable *truth* of propositional statements. Knowledge was being made dependent (and might even be called a *dependant!*) on the making of true statements. But this, I thought, was putting the cart before the horse. The verbal—or other symbolic—statements of propositions are but the expression of something more basic, more fundamental, namely the mind's self-transcending power of being cognitively aware of a world which is not itself. It was not of course denied that for a great deal of knowledge it is of the utmost importance that it should be expressed explicitly in verbal statements, and could not be clearly grasped as knowledge without it. But the mind's transcendent power, the everyday mystery, of being able to *know*, in the wide sense of 'cognize', with infinite degrees of obscurity or clarity—this seemed basic and central. It was this living fact, of which statements are one kind of necessary articulation, deposited publicly, as it were, in an already shared public language, that was central.

So, instead of making knowledge a function of the truth of propositional statements, I turned it on its head and said that truth is a function, or attribute, or quality, of the mind's living cognitive apprehension of the world. I used the metaphor of 'prehension' or cognitive grasping. Physically, when we stretch out to grasp something, we may get a firm hold of it, or we may fumble and slip. The metaphor of cognitive prehension was meant to suggest that when it was working efficiently, the character of the cognitive prehension was, in some degree at any rate, 'true', and when working inefficiently, in various degrees false. Truth and falsity were, I suggested, finally characters of the efficiency of the living self-transcending cognitive activity of mind apprehending its object. The truth of propositions was dependent on and in part derivative from that. Truth was, therefore, ultimately adverbial rather than adjectival, the character of a self-transcending mental activity rather than of a statement—however important in the realm of propositional knowledge statements may be. It seems better, on any inclusive view of knowledge, to speak of the truthful cognizing of mind, than of mind's cognition of truth, as though truth were wholly a character of propositions conforming with fact. In many contexts, in the contexts of propositional knowledge, it would of course be absurd to boggle at the statement that propositions are 'true'. But it is shorthand, and elliptical, and in a wider perspective of knowledge it can be most misleading. Truth is, to repeat, an adverb of knowing rather than, finally, an adjective of the relation between propositions and fact, however prevalent the articulation of truth in propositional-statement form may be.

One crucial advantage of this kind of view is that it opens up the way to understanding different kinds of knowing and knowledge. The propositional approach is, I think, parochial in that it accounts for only one kind of knowledge—though the 'parish' is admittedly a very large one! Direct acquaintance- and experience-knowledge, direct intuition, acknowledged formally though they may be, are not, in the propositionally conventional sense of knowledge, first-class citizens.

It is perhaps here relevant to repeat, in wider context, what was said in Chapter I.

If 'knowledge' indeed depended on being able to say justifiably something that is true, it would discount huge areas of what we all recognize to be knowledge-claims. Apart from knowledge-how, now accepted, there is Polanyi's[5] 'tacit' knowledge, where we know far more than we can say. This is a knowledge of things resting on an interpretative framework functioning a-critically. We can have topological knowledge of a town, or we can recognize a face, or a family resemblance, without being able—

either at the time, and sometimes not at all—to articulate it verbally. Then there is the knowledge of intrinsic values with which we are particularly concerned here—aesthetic, moral, personal. There is a vast literature *about* values. But any profitable talk about them presupposes direct experiential knowledge of them, immediate insights, conative and affective as well as cognitive, in fact personal insights in which these work together as a single whole. These insights can up to a point be described and shared imaginatively, but only significantly with those who have already experienced something of the same kind of thing. What is being referred to in any description is something which has to be known in independent intuition. In the case of the arts, for example, I shall in the next chapter try to show the impossibility of expressing artistic meaning, as such, in propositional statements.

The position I have been defending here is that language is an instrument, an expressive manifestation, of living cognitiveness, a basic form of life; and a major instance of this is judgement (personal judgement) expressed in the symbols of propositions which are always abstractions from reality. What is stated is always one abstraction (of many possible), an abstraction based on, picked out from, the concrete reality. Therefore propositions, however many they may be, can never state, or *say*, the reality. The reality has to be 'shown' in concrete experience which is cognitive-conative-affective.

In propositions about matters of fact the necessary background of concrete experience—e.g. sense experience or common logical sense— usually raises no problems. In judgements of value—moral, aesthetic, personal—problems do arise because in any basic experience of value, feeling is necessarily involved, and questions of subjectivity and objectivity immediately arise. This, particularly if one is seduced by a culture which assumes that only true propositional statements can yield knowledge, can lead to a general scepticism about *knowledge* of values being possible at all. On the other hand, although judgements of value cannot claim the same degree of certainty of many propositional statements of fact, secured by their abstractness, from an educational point of view the holistic requirements of the making of personal value judgements are a peculiarly valuable challenge to growing personalities.

4. Propositions, and knowledge of art

In the next chapter I shall examine an unusual view, that the arts are a *unique* form of knowledge, *and* that this form is the form of propositional statements. This is a position developed some years ago by Professor P.H. Hirst in two papers.[6]

It may seem odd to devote a large part of a chapter to what is an unusual position. I do so because Professor Hirst's writings on the 'forms of knowledge' have been very influential (and very controversial) in philosophy of education, because of the brilliant clarity of his writing, but particularly here for the way in which he develops his views to their logical limits. He puts what seem to be two contradictory statements side by side. They are: (a) that the arts 'constitute an area in which we have a knowledge of a *unique* form' (italic mine), and (b) that the paradigm of knowledge is exemplified 'in statements like $2 + 2 = 4$; water boils at $100\,°C$; the cat sat on the mat'. Professor Hirst remarks that 'this may well be the least interesting, indeed the least important and valuable, aspect of the arts ... In art, enjoyment may be more important than anything else.'

I agree with these comments. But if enjoyment is important, as it is, what *kind* of enjoyment is it, and how does it arise? If art gives knowledge of a kind, may not the 'unique' kind of knowledge that it is, its significance, arise from a unique kind of insightful enjoyment?

Through criticism of Hirst I shall positively suggest, in the next chapter, and in Chapter V, that this is so, and how it is so.

Chapter IV
Propositional Statements, and Knowing in the Arts

Professor Hirst affirms his agreement with the common analysis of knowledge-that: 'A believes a proposition: the proposition is true: and A is justified in believing it is true'. And he says that the observable features of art 'are used as symbols, have meaning, can be seen as making artistic statements and judged true or false just as words and sentences can be used to make scientific statements'.[1] Then there is his (already quoted) suggestion that this knowledge may be 'less important' than 'enjoyment' of art. But suppose (as I have commented) that 'a most important' thing about art *is* the enjoyment, the direct experience of it as an ongoing experience, suppose that this is taken in a broad sense of enjoyment central to the *knowledge* of art? If this turns out to be so, will there not be something artificial, perhaps downright wrong, in totally excluding (as we shall see he does) from consideration of the 'knowledge' of art all factors of 'coming to know', 'common occurrent experience' (which would include enjoyment), 'existential elements', 'acquaintance', and so on, and instead concentrating exclusively on 'knowledge of a propositional or statement kind'.[2] These are the questions we have to ask.

1. Propositional, and aesthetic, uses of language

In the objectively mathematical, scientific, or other conceptual knowledge with which Hirst is concerned in most of his writing, involvement in the experiences of knowledge is not, as we have said, of central importance, though there always is some involvement. One wants such knowledge to be dry and cold. But in the arts it is quite different. Even if it is true (the at present open question) that knowledge of art is a form of knowing-that, or 'knowledge of what is expressed in true statements',[3] could the total importance for human beings of art as a unique form of knowledge ever be compassed, or even indicated, in this partial and statement-bound account of knowledge?

Most of Hirst's paper turns on his deliberately exclusive attention to knowledge-that, 'propositional knowledge or knowledge of what is expressed in true statements', and turns on his view that 'knowledge with the direct object' can be analysed into 'knowing-how' and 'knowing-that'. I agree with him that 'knowledge with the direct object' presupposes knowledge-how and (at any mature stage) knowledge-that. (I also agree with his rejection of Russell's particular version of 'knowledge by acquaintance'.) On the other hand, although it can certainly be questioned whether acquaintance isolated from everything else is 'knowledge' in a comprehensive sense of the word, there is the direct intuitive factor in all knowledge, given explicit differentiation of content by knowledge-that. Applied to art, this means that aesthetic knowledge of art always presupposes direct acquaintance-experience of works of art, of content, discriminated with the aid of knowledge-that and knowledge-how. I certainly deny Hirst's contention in his earlier paper that all knowledge is analysable into, or reducible to, knowledge-that. As far as knowledge of art goes, we cannot leave out direct experience-knowledge, and hope to understand what we are talking about.

In the ordinary use of language and in its use in an art such as poetry, there is an established connection between words and meaning. In poetry, the ordinary relationship may be taken for granted, in so far as poetry uses words in an ordinary straightforward sense. But the connection between words and meaning as used in poetry is much more complex, and intimate in a special way of its own. In poetry there is the special attention to words. In ordinary statements (of fact, or of relation between concepts, etc.), the instrumental function of the language is to express ideas as clearly, literally and unambiguously as possible, in a rule-governed way. If the ideas are clearly expressed, the use of this language has been accomplished, and we do not pay particular attention to the words or word structure except in so far as it is necessary to grasp clear ideas. But in poetry, though words are necessarily instrumental too, that to which they are instrumental is quite different, and the form of those very particular sounding words, their weight, rhythm, balance, dynamics, have an importance and must be attended to in a way which is not necessarily appropriate when we are using language to achieve clarity of ideas—unless indeed we happen, as we may do sometimes, to be attending to these aesthetically. In saying this, I do not of course mean that in poetry we attend only to the sensuous form of meaningful words. We attend too to poetic images and ideas which the words express and embody in their sounding structure. But it is the meaning embodied in this very particular and individual perceived structure which is the focus of aesthetic attention, and this is very different from the recognition of the clear meaning which ordinary linguistic statements express. I am not of course arguing that because clarity of statement in this sense is the aim of ordinary language, poetic meaning is unclear or obscure. But since attention to (and feeling of) the form of the sounding words and images is attention to part of the poetic meaning, the words of poetry, though instrumental, are not instrumental as they are when the aim is clear statement. This makes the notion of 'poetic clarity' a different sort of thing from conceptual or factual clarity. Again, it is open-ended. Whereas in the use of ordinary language, ambiguity is a defect (puns, for instance, are 'out'), poetic language, as we all know, makes much use of what William Empson called 'ambiguity'. Empson discerned seven types.[4] David R. Olsen[5] prefers the word 'polysemy', as I do. Ambiguity refers to situations in which we have to choose between alternative meanings. But in poetic polysemy the meanings are fused together. In fact, the good poet not only means what he/she says (sometimes with this special deliberate 'ambiguity'), but says what he/she means in saying it, and saying it in one, literally untranslatable, way. (There is a special problem of the translation of poetry into another language which is quite different from that of the translation of science or philosophy.)

Each art (and varieties within each art) is different from the others, and some of the things I have just said about poetry could be applied to other arts—though arts like pure music, at one end of the scale, and the novel at the other, require special consideration. But there is one generalization which is true of art of every kind, and that is that every work of art is an existent embodiment of *value*.

Professor Hirst believes that there are some close parallels between works of art and statements (for example, scientific), though there are admitted differences. I want now to point out a difference, which I think is vital. Statements of the kind that express knowledge-about or knowledge-that are factual in nature—'it is the case that . . .' This is so when they are true statements of conceptual relations or even about value. To state that one ought to tell the truth, that respect for persons is good, is to make general statements *about* value. But none of the statements, as statements, are in themselves, as they stand, values. Of course all statements made by human beings have some instrumental value. We do not utter them without some interest, point or purpose. Even such an uninteresting statement as 'the cat is on the mat' is made for the sake of illustrating a point, and to make a clear point in argument has some value in itself (though it is in turn instrumentally valuable for further argument, etc.). But a statement of fact is, as statement, about as impersonal and value-free as anything could be. On the other hand, suppose we call a work of art a 'statement' (or say that it contains 'statements'). If we do, we shall be using 'statement', I think, in a metaphorical sense (as seeming to assert, to make a positive affirmation); but it is a possible one. One could call a first brush-stroke or complex of brush-strokes on canvas, a 'statement'. We do sometimes speak of 'statements' in music, and I suppose an actor or dancer in action could be said to make 'statements' sometimes. But if so, they are statements which, within the experience of art, are objects or existents possessing inherent value. They are presentations. They are made by the artist as expressive embodiments of value, and enjoyed by us as value-objects. Even when the medium is literary, the verbal statements, even if they happen to be true to life in the ordinary sense, are never just statements of fact. This is obviously true of poetic declarations; it is true of the novel too, although the novel is a borderline and limiting case. If one takes a single example in poetry, an extract from Matthew Arnold's 'Dover Beach':

> The sea of faith
> Was once, too, at the full, and round earth's shore
> Lay like the folds of a bright girdle furled;
>   But now I only hear
> Its melancholy, long, withdrawing roar,
>   Retreating . . .

We know very well that Arnold was talking about (and in a sense stating) the then effect of new discoveries in science upon the then religious faith. But the words of the poem, read aloud intelligently, must be read with a *feeling* for the values (positive and negative), feeling finely embodied in the sound, rhythm, balance, direction and varying weight of the subtly constructed patterns of words. The same is true, *mutatis mutandis*, of other arts. The supposed 'statements' of music, drama, painting, sculpture, dance . . . are created to be enjoyed aesthetically for their values as aesthetically embodied in those particular and individual forms, which have to be attended to for their own sakes, for themselves.

'Enjoyed' does not mean that it is all for 'pleasure', though pleasure of different kinds may be involved. (But we can 'enjoy' tragedy.) It is intelligent enjoyment which includes all the different aspects of consciousness, cognitive, conative, affective.

2. Aesthetic knowledge, and experience

What is essential, then, is that, in order to come to know art, we should attend to it as embodiment of value (or value-embodied), and cognitively feel it as value. This is why Professor Hirst's initial exclusion: 'I am not concerned with the experience of coming to know' is so question-begging, and disastrous for the understanding of aesthetic *knowledge*. Menhuin, in a master-class, said to a pupil: 'Until the current flows from the toes to the fingers . . . and you feel the weight and movement of the body . . .' you won't quite 'get' the music. Again: 'Don't try for accuracy before you get the *feeling* of the motion . . .' He was talking partly of know-how, and of a 'knowledge' which in this case demands the most sensitive feeling. An enormous amount of knowledge-that is required to know music intellectually, but without acquaintance through feeling it is so much dead wood—rather like 'having all knowledge' and being, without '*caritas*', nothing. Love in art, discriminating and perceptive, is not everything; but without it there is no aesthetic knowledge of art at all. This is the very heart of the matter. In this respect, knowledge of an art 'statement' is about as unlike knowledge of a matter-of-fact statement as anything could be. The end-purpose is different. An art 'statement' can only have its aesthetic existence *as experienced, as felt, as known, by a person or persons*. A sonata, a poem, a picture, a dance, only fully exists (as distinct from written meaningful music, words, etc.) as it occurs in sophisticated aesthetic experience, or aesthetic experiences, of it. The felt experience of a personal subject is, I suggest, organic to its existence. This by no means implies that art is 'merely private, merely subjective', but only that subjective experience and cognitive feeling is part of its full existence, and centrally relevant.

To sum up this part of the argument: the affirmation that art is 'statement of what is the case' (of facts) seems wholly irrelevant. Examples such as $2 + 2 = 4$, 'Water boils at $100\,°C$.', 'the cat sat on a mat', from mathematics, science, or common sense, are as unlike what art 'says' as anything could be. The 'enjoyment' which Hirst mentions as possibly the 'most important' thing about art may well be one of the most important things about it if, *and only if*, the 'enjoyment' is interpreted in a way which does justice to what the arts really are and do. If the arts were statements of what is the case, the enjoyment of *that* would be limited indeed. The *discovery* of new facts by great scientists is no doubt to those scientists who discover them a deep joy. The statement of the facts, once discovered and established, is less so. Though we accept facts once established and state them when relevant, no one just goes on stating facts for enjoyment in itself. But we *do* go on, and we return again and again, to the great works of art—to Bach, Mozart, Rembrandt, Cézanne, Marlowe, Shakespeare ... Some of them, the literary arts for example, may indeed state 'facts' about the world and human nature. But if they do so, this is their beginning and not their end. The facts are not *faits accomplis*; they are challenges to fresh explorations of human experience, where fact is saturated with value.

I have been saying, then, that Hirst's preoccupation with statements to the exclusion of any consideration of aesthetic experience and enjoyment of art disqualifies his account of art as a form of knowledge. But this is not simply a lack of *consideration* of direct aesthetic experience of art as an essential aspect of the knowledge and understanding of art. Whatever Hirst may think of the importance of the enjoyment of art, there is implied a downright denial that direct experience ('enjoyable' experience) of art could constitute knowledge of art at all. For he denies that any direct experience of any kind can be accounted 'knowledge'. Direct experience is 'non-knowledge'.

3. Direct knowledge, art knowledge, and conceptual interpretation

Reaffirming the common propositional account of knowledge, Hirst says that 'what it is that is known cannot be identified, even by the knowers, let alone others, apart from the use of ... concepts' expressed in the propositions.[6] He goes on to say that both the knowledge-how and 'knowledge with a direct object' are 'involved with', or 'closely related to' knowledge-that. So far as ordinary propositional knowledge goes, I have (as I have said) no quarrel with this. But I have denied that it applies in any straightforward way to experience-knowledge of art, and I now also deny the assertion that knowledge with the direct object is always reducible[7] 'to know-that and know-how, *plus* another non-knowledge element'. Of direct-object experience—in this case, of *music*—Hirst writes:

Beyond the know-that and the know-how that are implied, there always seems to be included too a reference to some direct experience of the object on which certain of the basic elements of know-that and know-how rest. It is this element of personal experience as the foundation on which know-that and know-how rest that is being highlighted in many cases when we speak of knowledge with a direct object. If this is so, then knowledge of this last kind is analysable into some complex of elements of knowledge of the other two kinds plus an assertion of direct experience of the object concerned. If this is granted then it will of course follow that different cases of knowledge will ultimately be distinguishable from each other only by reference to the elements of knowledge-that which are involved.[8]

There are two points at issue here. One concerns knowledge generally, the other the experience-knowledge of art.

First, there is this analytic habit of divisiveness, of compartmental thinking. It is symbolized in Hirst's metaphor of the 'base' or 'foundation' of 'non-knowledge', direct experience, upon which the structure of authentic or proper knowledge is 'built'. The quite valid distinction between two phases of knowing is conceived as a separation, and the relation between the two an external one. But the relation is internal and, if metaphors are in order at all, it is better to think of knowledge growing and developing continuously from roots rather than as additive in discrete layers; foundation, then superstructure. But, as I have already urged, direct 'knowledge' as 'non-knowledge' distorts the facts of experience. When we taste an onion, smell a rose, see a tree or a landscape, encounter a person ... do not qualities and structures impinge, and are they not discriminated directly without necessarily any of the 'labelling'[9] to which Hirst refers and which he says is necessary in order to 'identify'? Very often of course, because of past experience, labels are implicit though, not explicit. But that the content of many impingements not only *are* not, but often *cannot*, be labelled, gives not the slightest reason for saying that we do not *know* qualities and structures which we directly experience. No one but philosophers 'bewitched' by a traditional and contemporary *idée fixe* arguing in the interests of a limited theory would insist that all is 'non-knowledge' (or non-cognitive) till we have done the labelling. Hirst says that 'what it is that is known cannot be *identified*' apart from the use of labelling concepts. This is only true if, tautologically, 'identification' just means labelling. But in directly perceiving qualities or structures are we not directly cognizing things which each already have, and are recognized to have, their own identities? Is not 'labelling' identification, the labelling of entities which must be supposed as existing already, and which we cognize directly?

In the case of art knowledge, it is quite simply false to say that we do not *know* anything till we have identified it conceptually by labelling, implicitly or explicitly. The fact is that in the instance of music not only do we not come to know what we immediately perceive musically by conceptually labelling it: we *cannot* know this individual piece of music by labelling it conceptually because as an *individual* piece of music it cannot be labelled conceptually. Of course, there are an indefinite number of facts about music, known to musicians and musicologists, and music can be talked about conceptually like anything else: it has a complicated vocabulary. And discourse about music can retroactively affect the experience and understanding of music—though it does not necessarily do so. (See Chapter V, Section 3.) But each work of music, and each part of each work, as actually played or listened to musically in musical experience, is uniquely individual, is known as individual, however true it may be at another level of language, that it is a 'sonata' or a 'fugue', or anything else. *This* music as heard musically cannot, cannot logically, because it is individual, be captured (or labelled) under any *general* category or concept. This is always true; but it is vividly seen in the case when people who are naturally musical but totally ignorant of musical terms hear a piece of music and are moved by the unnamed musical character of what they hear. They have no 'knowledge' of music; but is what they have just completely 'non-knowledge'? Of course it is not. Moreover, if they had a vast vocabulary of music but could not musically hear *this*, what would their 'musical knowledge' be worth?

4. Occurrent cognition, and art

The division between knowledge-that and direct knowledge is compounded by Hirst's denial that the word 'knowledge' can label an *occurrent* experience of any kind, but that knowledge is always a dispositional state. 'I know that $2 + 2 = 4$, how to ride a bicycle, when I am asleep.'[10] The affirmation is true enough; but the denial seems arbitrary. A great deal at least of our dispositional knowledge depends on there having been occurrent experience of knowing and coming to know. Coming to know has a developmental history, again some of it propositional, some not, and which feeds into the dispositional.

Whatever account one gives of cognitive development, surely these events and changes are all *cognitive* events and changes? This seems to apply to all kinds of knowing and knowledge; and the occurrences, the cognitive occurrences and cognitive experiences, seem to be necessary conditions for the achievement or attainment of dispositional knowledge. Why, except in the interests of consistency with one restrictive definition of 'knowledge', should this natural usage be denied? Hirst says: 'The experiences of coming to know may be varied, e.g. visual perceptions, hearing of statements, acts of intellectual judgement, practical activities. But, again, none of these is knowing as such.'[11] If by 'knowing as such' is meant dispositional knowledge of truths firmly established, then the statement is, analytically, true. But in epistemology, in the history of the theory of knowledge, the story of knowing and knowledge cannot be confined to one phase of it, however important—to the final *establishment* in a disposition of the mind, of one particular (propositional) kind of knowledge. Isn't the affirmation that it is, philosophically dictatorial?

The view that knowledge is always dispositional and never occurrent is completely implausible when applied to the arts. If we think of music, for instance, it is true that experienced musicians have masses of dispositional knowledge. But they acquired this dispositional knowledge in the long course of their experience, of which, many, many, occurrents were intrinsic parts. Into their dispositional knowledge of music, the accumulation of concrete memories of occurrent musical experience is fused and relevantly transformed, ready to be called into new occurrent operations in the performing, or hearing, of the music they know. And this is not just a flat repetition of dispositionally established fact. Every living performance, or hearing, is in part a rediscovery, a coming to fresh musical knowing, of aspects of new meaning. I know $2 + 2 = 4$; and it would perhaps be pedantic, when I repeat it, to say that my knowing is occurrent. It is flat matter of fact, no discovery. Not so with music. My dispositional knowledge of music is not merely general knowledge of fact, knowledge-that. It is concrete knowledge-of, of individuals, knowledge which possessed the whole person, and it needs to be renewed and added to in fresh experiences, occurrent experiences. There is *no* way of acquiring dispositional knowledge of music except by repeated occurrent experiences of it.

5. Language and the fine arts

The general sense of what I have been saying is happily corroborated and supplemented in two articles on language and art by Harold Osborne and Leslie R. Perry respectively, which appeared since this chapter was first written.[12] I shall refer to some supporting passages.

In sometimes referring to art as a 'language', I have consistently employed inverted commas, for indiscriminately to apply the term 'language' to the arts is highly misleading. Osborne uses the term 'metaphor'.

> Linguistic communication brings about a four-term relationship. There is a *speaker* who communicates, intentionally or sometimes involuntarily. Language, written or spoken, is his instrument, the *vehicle* which carries his meaning. There is the *message* that is communicated. And there is the *hearer* who receives and interprets the communication, apprehending the message. Language, the vehicle which carries the meaning, is not identical with the message communicated or with the message intended to be communicated. For languages can be translated; the same message can be translated in different words.[13]

Sometimes language is defective. There are relatively few words to express the subtleties and nuances of emotional states, or of colours.

The common distinction between representational and non-representational arts is important here. It can be interpreted as a distinction between arts which are, and arts which are not, referential. The non-referential arts (for example, music) do not fit into the root conception of language outlined.

> There is no message and no vehicle in any straightforward sense of these words. I believe that no useful result can come of trying to fit them into the straitjacket of the linguistic metaphor by unusual interpretations or forced analogies. The referential arts, on the other hand, do conform in a general way to the pattern of linguistic communication ... But there are pretty fundamental ways in which they differ from the linguistic model ... In everyday intercourse between man and man it is primarily the message which interests us. The function of the linguistic vehicle is limited to ensuring communication of the message from person to person ... In our commerce with the arts the position is reversed. Aesthetic appreciation is a cognitive activity, an exercise of enlarged perception leading to a state of expanded awareness. Its proper object is the vehicle, the work of art ... We are not primarily concerned with a work of art as a vehicle to carry a message, but in the thing itself as it is presented to perception. This is contrary to the fundamental nature of language. In linguistic communication the vehicle is *transparent*, we see 'through' it to the message it carries ... But when we take up an aesthetic attitude, the vehicle becomes *opaque*.[14]

This is true even in the literary arts whose very substance is language. We are not interested in the poem simply as a vehicle communicating a message of the poet. We are interested in the whole complex structure of meanings inherent in it, including the rhythm and the music of the language, and the penumbra of secondary associated meanings which words can carry. In the referential arts we are not concerned with matter-of-fact truth, but with the feel and savour of things true or imaginary, thus expanding and enriching our experience.

Nor are the referential—or the non-referential—arts structurally symbolic systems like modes of expression in ordinary language.

> Languages are composed of units of expression, technically called elements of discourse, which are grouped into patterns of sentences, etc., according to rules of syntax. Communication is achieved by selecting a particular pattern of elements among the possible patterns within the constraints imposed by the rules of the language. The complex patterned structure so formed functions as a vehicle carrying a message. This process is made possible because individual words have referential (including grammatical, associative, and emotional) meanings, which often acquire added sharpness and precision when the words are combined into linguistic structures. These are the building blocks of language. But music and the visual arts have no such building blocks. Their structure is organized on a different principle. They are organized as multi-level structures, each level consisting of sub systems which are wholes with regard to their parts and parts within the larger wholes. And each part is an integrated whole whose properties cannot be reduced to those of its parts.[15]

The term 'grammar' is commonly used nowadays to cover the rules of phonology, syntax and semantics, but not the lexicon. 'My contention has been that fine art has no lexicon and therefore no grammar.'[16]

Perry observes that communication in ordinary language between members of the public

> is a *generalizing* thing, relying upon the assumption that our minds closely resemble each other in order to assign standard meanings in language. But individuals, as Dahrendorf (in *Homo Sociologicus*) has remarked, are not solely specimens of *homo sociologicus*, dealing in roles and conventions of conduct. They have an inner and *personal* state of mind . . . The *public* use and the *private* use [of language] both produce language structures and usages, but the types of pressure they produce are quite different: as a social instrument, language tends to be generalized and precise; but as handled by individuals, it is under constant pressure to alter its meanings, and it is obscure and inexact. When it comes to the arts and other areas of the inner mind which are in the borderland of articulation, the pressure on language becomes extreme, and it finally breaks down as a means of communication.[17]

Perry stresses the point I have also stressed, the current domination of *proposition*-based language over *judgements*.

Propositions are an abstraction from judgements, and this abstraction consists in stripping away the existential content in order to give judgement a
homogeneous formalized structure ... The important thing about full discourse on knowledge is not its propositional structure but its judgemental
one, which admits the existential content and grapples with its individual
aspect ... Language is a sign system for public and general communication
and a symbol system for an art like poetry. In so far as symbols carry with
them an embodied evocative power over feelings and motives, they are more
than signs conveying a meaning not their own. In so far as cognitively based
sign systems have primacy at present, the problem of the relation of the
aesthetic symbol to the linguistic sign becomes acute, the more so because
aesthetic symbols are post-language inventions for everyone and may be
suffused with language and sign-based experience as well as require it for
understanding.[18]

And, broadly speaking

In ordinary perception, the conceptual nexus is directed towards the external
world, whereas in the arts it is frequently centred on an interior world that is
to be communicated and perceived.[19]

The stock words we have for personal experiences, feelings, attitudes
and the rest

allow a latitude of interpretation even to come close to being specific enough.
Hence we have to apply immediately to that art object which is the outcome of
the artist's feeling complex and yield ourselves to our reponse to it.[20]

And,

many artists would say that their cognitive experiences are insignificant
compared with their affective ones.[21]

(I would, of course, say that, in a broader sense of 'cognitive', these
'affective' experiences *are* 'cognitive'.)

I do not apologize for quoting these two authors at some length. They
help to clarify what I think is the radical difference between the semantics of propositional statements and the semantics of the arts.

Chapter V
Understanding Art

This chapter takes up, and develops at a deeper level, some of the issues raised in Chapter IV—the personal involvement called forth by the arts, different uses of language in common speech and in the articulations of the arts, the contribution which conceptual thinking can make to the appreciation of the arts. All this was mainly vis-à-vis the view that genuine knowledge must be expressed in the propositional form.

Hence I shall try to bring out the nature of artistic intelligibility in contrast to that of science; the contrast between the individual and the universal. The creative processes of making and appreciating art, and the assimilation of general thinking into art are considered. So are some questions of interpretation, criticism, the art symbol, expression and embodiment.

1. Artistic and scientific intelligibility

One way of bringing out the unique nature of the art object and our understanding of its structure is to contrast it with scientific objects and our understanding of them, for the two can be said in many important aspects to be polar opposites. Science could be said, broadly, to be attempting to make sense of natural events by explaining their relationships within a system (ideally) of an assumed universal order. Scientific intelligibility, again broadly speaking, moves towards classifiability and prediction. 'Making sense' of art objects (or 'works of art'), on the other hand, is not achieved by 'explaining' it in relation to anything, any system, outside itself. And classification or prediction in any sense in which these terms resemble their use in science, has no place in the aesthetically experiential understanding of art.

Not in the 'aesthetically experiential understanding of art'. The bold, and bald, negatives need to be guarded by this emphasis on first-order experience. Second- and third-order approaches to art, criticism and aesthetics respectively can and often do discursively relate art to what is outside itself. Criticism, for example, may show works of art in their social or historical setting of culture and art history. Criticism or aesthetics may classify particular works as belonging to a school or style; and critics may be able to 'predict' in the sense that they may be able to say, for example, that this artist is likely to go on painting or writing or composing in the same general style, at least for a time. And they can, broadly, anticipate intelligently from direct experience of a work the likely general form in which, say, a piece of music will develop. (Baroque music would be a very obvious example.) But this is only a general, if intelligent, expectation. The kind of classification and prediction present in the sciences, where it can be said to specify instances as logically in a general class, and from that predict how the instances will behave—this has no place in aesthetic experience of art as such, because every authentic work of art is an individual and every part of it part of that individual and never merely an instance. As individual each authentic work is a new created thing, and its intelligibility is, aesthetically speaking, internal to itself, and cannot be 'explained' or justified by reference to a rationally ordered universal system external to itself.

Each work of art is 'new', not in the trifling sense in which each raindrop or each tick of the clock is new, but significantly and valuably new because it is a new creation with a form which requires a special act of experientially aesthetic attention in order to understand it as an individual with its own internally structured content.

There are two approaches from which one can view the significant newness of new creation. One is the approach of the creative artist, the other the approach of the spectator (listener, etc.) to given, presented art.

The *artist* never knows beforehand exactly the structure he or she is going to make and has no fixed rules to guide him/her towards this individual piece of making. Of course he/she has had previous experience of making, and a knowledge-of and knowledge-how of techniques potentially anticipatory; he/she has, too, habits and stylistic tendencies. But exactly how he/she is going to use these, and the potentialities of the medium in which he/she is working, he/she has often but vague and tentative feelings and ideas. There is neither a prefigured plan, derived or deduced from some given intelligible scheme, nor a fixed final plan operating teleogically towards which he/she can work. The final form of the particular painting, or poem, or sonata ... not only *is* not known beforehand by the creating artist: it *cannot* be known beforehand, because the form of a work of art as individual is not a *general* form or general pattern of structure into which the work will, as it were, fit, or be moulded by. The form of a particular and individual work is organically dependent on its parts as, in complementary fashion, the artistically-aesthetic meaning of the parts cannot be fully understood artistically except as functioning in artistically-organic relation to all other parts and to the whole. There are, of course, general artistic forms which have general names—the sonnet, the fugue—and the artist can say beforehand that he/she is going to make something in a particular form of that general kind. But the 'form', spoken of quite legitimately in that way, is the form in quite a different sense from the individual form of *this* work, which is creatively built up in a temporal process and does not exist as an artistic form until the actual building up is complete. There is form as a general concept, and form as existential.

And this latter, if it 'comes off' as in genuine works of art, major or minor, it does, is something which can truly be called a 'creation'. The words 'creative' and 'creativity' have been so bandied about as to have become almost meaningless clichés. But in good or great art something genuinely new and important is brought into the world: and in a sense it remains new; or, if that is thought too paradoxical, unique and individual, long after it was first made—and even forever.

Carl R. Hausman describes it well: the process, and the paradox, of the creative articulation of the artist, the discovery which happens in the making of art. The artist

> formulates his plan at the same time ... that he sees what is required to complete the process he started ... He must generate a necessitated product which is not necessitated by anything given to the creator with which he can generate it. In short, the creator must act as an agent which is a cause without a prior cause, a cause which causes itself.[1]

This sounds thoroughly irrational; and many people do call art irrational. But it is only 'irrational' if 'rational' means something like 'logically deduced'. But that is both far too sweeping and too narrow: it would condemn scientific thinking itself as 'irrational' in its inductive aspect—and indeed somewhere about the 1920s or 1930s current talk about the 'scandal of induction' meant exactly this. But why, because we cannot know directly as they occur the tacit processes of the inductive leap towards a new hypothesis in scientific thinking, or the 'artistic leap' in art creation, should we call them 'irrational' because they are not logically deduced? The great 'creative' scientific discovery in theoretical science is discovery of a new phase in the concept of natural order, rational order. The great creative discovery of the artist is the discovery of a new form, a new order of the structure of an individual work of art. Who shall say that the order of a great sonata, or painting, or poem, creatively discovered in this way is wholly 'irrational', and in achievement is *not* a 'rational' order, unless indeed on the assumption that deductive logic is the one and only authentic model of the rational?

Hausman, quoted above, has other illuminating things[2] to say about this mysterious thing, artistic creation. One of them is an application of the Platonic, and later Christian-theological, ideas of agape and eros, to art-creation. I shall be returning to these concepts later in another context in Chapters VI and VII. Meantime I will only remind readers that agape in Christian theology and religion means the outgoing love of God directed towards all persons, sinner and saint alike, and is 'uncaused' in the sense that the love is not evoked by any good or attractive qualities in the persons loved, but is concern for their good and well-being. Eros, on the other hand, is 'caused' love, caused by the qualities in the beloved, dependent on the beloved for fulfilment. The denotation of eros is of course much wider than the 'erotic' in the sexual sense.

(I shall expound this partly in my own words and partly in Hausman's, because I am not wholly certain I have grasped him completely.)

The idea that creative acts may be driven by love in the sense of eros should not seem surprising. Artists, though they have often to endure anguish and painful effort, have a passionate love for their work, and when they make one, can be overcome with a joy like the joy after consummated love. But the kind of love which operates in artistic creation cannot adequately be described exclusively in terms of eros. The basis of the dynamic thrust of eros is the attraction of the consummation which is desired. But in the creation of art, the nature of the end desired is not fully known beforehand: and if it were known beforehand the process of making art would not be creative, but would be simply determined by its initial direction, without varying as the working proceeds. As predetermined, there would be no novelty in the intelligible structure of the outcome.

Eros by itself is, then, not enough to account for the creative and self-determining character of art. Hausman (drawing some of his ideas from A.N. Whitehead's *Adventures of Ideas* and *Process and Reality*) points out that the *telos* or end of the (art) process itself changes; hence it could not *pre*structure the process. At the beginning of the creative process, as we have seen, the artist envisages only a vague and at best partially determinate end. I spoke earlier in a metaphor of a sort of 'dialogue' between the artist and his/her medium through which he/she discovers new meaning: and this is an essential factor in art making. Another factor in the dynamism of the artistic process is the outgoing drive of agape. As Hausman puts it: '. . . the creative act is not wholly uncontrolled. If there is serendipity, it is not sheer accident. The creator must not only exercise critical judgement in deciding what to accept and reject when possibilities occur to him, but he must also form, refine and integrate these, even if he knows only with a degree of imprecision what the final integration will be. And most important, he must assume responsibility for what he brings into being.'[3] Putting it in my own words: the motive finally is not of eros, seeking to fulfil itself by attaining a previsualized, predetermined goal, but is a kind of offering of itself by permitting creation to grow on its own terms. Artists both seek, and give themselves to, creation. The concern is not finally for self-fulfilment but for a new creature, the art which is yet to be. This concern is, I believe, an artist's moral responsibility. It requires its own very special kind of moral integrity; and the integrity of the art can hardly be had without it.

It is interesting, in this context, to compare the 'creative' discoveries of science with the 'creative' discoveries of art. It recalls the systematically generalized nature of science (see Chapter III). To call the genuine discoveries of the greatest scientists 'creative' is not, in my view, an honorific use of the word. Certainly the intuitive flashes of insight, and their products, are creative. But there is a difference, I think, in the final significance of the word as used in the two fields: and the difference turns on the individuality of each work of art. The theoretical discoveries of the great scientists are genuine creations in that they imaginatively 'feel after' and construct genuinely new and significant hypotheses. They are so significant because they can throw entirely new light on what was regarded as established systematic knowledge up to that point—of course in the tentative and 'open' sense of 'establishment' taken for granted among scientists. This is a crucial difference between science and art. Art as individual and new, both does not arise out of an established system of relatively logically and empirically coherent knowledge, and does not justify itself by illuminating any such system. Though a work of art always arises in a cultural context, as an individual it stands by and for itself, and its 'justification' is an internally aesthetic-artistic one. And so—if it is truly strong enough to stand on its own feet—it will remain. The great scientific 'creative' discovery is a great event in the life of the discoverer, and, for a while, in the life of contemporary scientists. But, as its significance finally is its bearing on systematic scientific understanding, the original discovery becomes resolved into that, and becomes part of the history of science. Of course it is true too that great works of art arise out of an artistic-cultural system, and that they too have influences recorded in history. But the history of art is of a very different kind from the history of science: if it is true at all that there is 'development' in art as time goes on, it is not true that new perspectives in art replace, or displace, older ones, in the way in which it can be said that new perspectives in science displace older ones. (See Chapter VIII, pp. 134–8.)

2. 'Intradiction'

If we look now at the process of the *appreciation* of works of art, there is again an interesting comparison to be made with scientific thinking and scientific prediction. Hausman invents the term 'intradiction' to label something which is in some ways like, but in other ways importantly different from, scientific prediction. He writes:

> I shall attempt to show that artistic appreciation includes a cognitive process which is something like predicting, but which must at the same time be clearly distinguished from prediction as it may occur in science and other forms of thought. The activity . . . will be called 'intradiction' . . . Thus I shall attempt to describe understanding in art so that it is possible to view the work of art and aesthetic experience as self-contained, immediate . . . and distinct from other forms of experience or thought, while at the same time recognising that analysis and interpretation need not do violence to the intuitive grasp of the art object.[4]

This understanding is parallel to the understanding of the creator: how all elements, including formal traits, meanings, themes, suggestions of mood . . . affect the characters of one another, how each part determines the nature of every other part, and the whole work determines and is determined by the parts, in a way which cannot be adequately stated in other symbols, or paraphrased. (Of course, full artistic understanding is an ideal.) The point of 'intradiction' is that a person who understands a work of art can, given recognition of some components of a work, anticipate (up to a point 'predict' . . . 'intradict') the presence of other components. It is a kind of *Gestalt* phenomenon, a very special one. The spectator, reader, listener ... if he/she has some knowledge and experience of a particular art, can have some *general* anticipatory feelings and ideas when beginning to experience a particular unfamiliar work. But it is strictly limited. Until he/she has been through the whole (at least once) he/she cannot know what exactly the parts are leading towards.

Take music, for example. Here, as with other arts, the reliability of anticipation has degrees, varying with powers of musical insight, previous knowledge of the art, and of the particular work. A musician with a musical understanding of *genres*, styles, etc., is more likely, on first hearing a piece of music, to be able to anticipate generally the sort of thing which will follow—though never its exact detail. (Indeed part of the joy of listening is being led on—and surprised!) Only after he/she has heard the piece through, once or more often, will he/she be able to predict with greater particularity. This is not just a matter of memory recall, but depends upon his/her understanding of the work as an aesthetically organic whole of parts. It is the sense of inner artistic necessity which gives coherent artistic understanding of parts in relation to one another in, and to, the whole. So the '*pre*diction', as far as it occurs, is a function of the '*intra*diction', which in turn is an immediate outcome of the aesthetic experience itself.

This being so, 'intra*diction*' seems not quite the right word. 'Intradiction' in the arts *may* break into speech at any time, perhaps more often in literary arts than in music. But it need not do so; and in any case the 'diction' will be of a different nature from the clear symbolic factual *predictions* of the physical sciences. The actual process of what is being called 'intradiction' in art is more a *sense* of coming form, form-to-be, a feeling towards, in a total concrete experience of a piece of ongoing art, an as-yet-unknown artistic fulfilment.

But this raises still another question. Intradiction may not always be articulated in speech, if we think of intradiction as taking place during the process of actually experiencing a work of art. But in art analysis, and in criticism, we certainly do articulate our thoughts in speech or writing, using discursive language. Discursive language belongs, we know, to a different order of understanding from the direct intuitive understanding of art, which is not, as has been argued, a 'language'—or if so, only metaphorically. But in the comprehensive understanding of the nature of art, and in the understanding of particular works of art, discursive language, which traffics in abstractions and universals, makes its indispensable contribution. And the question is, 'How does it do so?' How can analysis, or the talk of criticism, often dry and essentially charged with abstractions, come to operate beneficially on the so different concrete and intuitive experience of art? How can it illuminate our direct aesthetic-artistic understanding? Again I will take the example of music.

3. The metamorphosis of concepts in musical experience

In the absorbed experience of music, whether in listening or performing, the overt consciousness of verbally linguistic distinctions is hardly, if at all, present. At other times, we can read statements like the following. 'The fugue is throughout in various kinds of Double and Triple Counterpoint, and its Episodes are derived one from another and recapitulated symmetrically . . . Episode 1 is in bars 5 and 6 (before entry of the third voice), and combines the main figure of the subject with an important new counterpoint.' (Tovey on Fugue II, Book I of the Forty-Eight.[5]) The words used here are general and abstract, and the statements describe the structure of one particular fugue. The very general terms are abstractions picked out from musical experience and practice, and are, necessarily, stated seriatim. As such, they belong to a modality clearly distinguishable, entirely different, from the operation of 'double and triple counterpoint . . .' as these actually occur in musical performance. But to be understood *musically*, say by the performer, they must be thought, felt, imagined, played, as *immanent*, as embodied, in the actual flowing music itself. The *musicological* thinking is in its nature skeletal, the product of analysis into bits, expressed in chunks of abstract language related to one another conceptually (though always, if they are properly understood, in the background context of actual music). The *musical* thinking is not abstract thinking but concrete thinking. Abstract concepts of structure, in this phase of experience, are no longer in the focus of attention. They have become assimilated, always in the *personal* mind of the musician, so that they operate musically without focally conscious attention to them as general abstractions. There are, it is true, stages in learning a new piece of music when they (together with other factors such as techniques) have to be focally attended to. But when there is mastery, the attention to abstractions and techniques has done its work, and they are forgotten, as such. In this sense art is 'concept-free', as Kant said. In another it is not. It is important that analysis should have done its work; this is one thing which distinguishes intelligent and knowledgeable musicianship. The change from abstract musicological discourse to concrete musical thinking-feeling-performing is a *metamorphosis*. The effect of detached thinking about music is not lost, does not disappear. But through its assimilation into the personal musical mind it is changed in form and becomes part of musical seeing, thinking, understanding, feeling, moving—a ceremony of musical devotion. The abstract thinking, as such, has effaced itself, and, in a sense, has died. But in doing so it has given itself to a new concrete individual life, of *this* piece of music. In abstract thinking one thinks of things of certain *kinds*, certain *kinds* of thing. In art one attends to a *this* (which has assimilated many 'kinds' into its own creative organization).

Tovey says, in advice to players: 'The initial tempo should be so moderate and the touch and pedalling so light that the listener can suspect far more harmonic detail than one chord in the bar.'[6] Menuhin says, 'It can sound like scales and arpeggios—but in Beethoven there are really no scales and arpeggios: there is a flow.' Again Menuhin, 'One must realise the significance of this passage in relation to the whole work ... Don't underline that phrase; think, then forget, and having thought you will do it differently ... The music in this concerto is cumulative, like a snowball.'

4. Interpretation, in music and literature

Both originative and receptive modes of artistic discovery imply interpretation—which is quite different from scientific interpretation where the lucid statement of an hypothesis is definite and understood by those who do understand it. The interpretation of art is not a clear statement and requires, in the first instance anyhow, some personal, private and part-subjective approach—though it can subsequently be discussed publicly. This can be seen if we look at two forms of artistic interpretation, music and literature. First, music.

Here there is again the twofold scene, the original artist's interpretation of his/her own work (how he/she 'sees' it), and the performer's or listener's interpretation of the work as materially and symbolically given. The composer's interpretation we do not as a rule know, and often cannot know. There are exceptions, as when living composers play or conduct their own work and are heard by discerning contemporaries. But even this might be changed in repeat performances by the same composer-performer. And apart from all this, we must not assume that the composer-performer's interpretation is the 'final' interpretation, or indeed that there must *be* a final and definitive interpretation.

What we have before us, what is immediately there, is a score written in conventionally given and conventionally understood public symbols, understood by all musicians, to be decoded, played, listened to by whoever is playing, listening, interpreting. 'Interpretation' here has two quite different meanings which must be clearly distinguished. One is commonplace, a technical skill of decoding the symbols, and in performance correctly playing the written notes. This is a necessary, but of course not sufficient, condition for interpretation in a second sense, which is a discerning musical (and generally, artistic) understanding of the literal decoded score. It is the nature of this which is the important issue here.

If we ourselves happen to be experienced musicians—critics or performers—we will have some considerable body of knowledge both artistic and factual which will help us to penetrate, though fallibly, the composer's approach to the composing and interpreting of the score, and to some limited extent (as I have suggested) the interpretation itself. We will know something of the genres, traditions, conventions, etc., which influenced the composer's approach, and which will help us to appreciate better the individual style. Such attention to compositions in their context is, of course, of very great importance.

But, however important, it is but a part of the musician's coming to understand and learning to interpret, which is a long job indeed. Jorge Bolet, in a television conversation, made the point in the following way. How long, he asked, does a composer take to create a particular work? A month? A year? . . . He/she then presumably goes on to other compositions. And how long does a professional performing artist spend studying and performing repeatedly a great artist's work? A lifetime. Bolet was unambiguously emphatic that musicians must, with everything they have, *study* the composer's work, and works. There must be no playing fast and loose with this: and study, ideally, means study of all the composer's works. But, he adds, a lifetime's study and performance may well reveal aspects of the music of which the composer may not have been aware. In fact, because a composition is a thing of many aspects, it would be strange if fresh aspects were not discovered in the deep and long study of musical works.

The quest for valid musical interpretation is in one, vitally important, sense a quest for *objectivity* of interpretation. Bolet seems to assume this, though he does not use the word. But it is the nature of this claimed objectivity which is the crucial question. About objectivity in decoding a conventionally written score there is no question. The score says (in its agreed language) 'a minor third in C major'. This is played on the piano. I can say, truly, with 'objective' truth, 'You played that correctly.' But 'objective' *musical* interpretation of a correctly decoded musical piece? That is a very different matter. This is so because while the 'interpretation' which in a banal sense decoding is, is literal, merely conventional, merely factual, where there is an exact point-to-point correspondence between symbols and material items of music—in musical interpretation there is no such thing. Musical interpretation is not the factual, merely technical skill of decoding—something which could be done efficiently by using one little part of the mind-and-body of a wholly unmusical person. Musical interpretation calls for an imaginative response, a response in which a whole person is potentially involved, intellectually in grasping musical structure, with sensitive feeling, cognitive and affective, conation and activity, sometimes emotion, all acting organically together as an apprehension of musical *values*, the 'emergent' or tertiary qualities of art.

The tertiary qualities of musical *materials* are the directly felt though strictly indescribable tertiary qualities of different sounds, tones, pitch, intervals, rhythms, timbres . . . The tertiary qualities of musical *elements* belong to these as ingredient in the musical organism. Again, 'life' words like 'sad' or 'gay' applied to music acquire new specifically concrete musical meaning. These tertiary qualities are inseparable from the response of personal subjects, functioning holistically. But this does not make them merely 'subjective'. As phenomena, appearances, data of human experience, they are, epistemologically, objective. As we all see the clouds on the mountains as 'lowering', the sea as 'peaceful' or 'angry', we see musical sequences as 'solemn', 'gay', or 'agitated'. In phenomenal experience, and certainly in aesthetic experience, these qualities, in any particular experience, *belong* to their phenomenal objects, though not as shape or weight belong to physical objects. We all share in using this kind of common language. That each subject must in his or her own private experience first come to apprehend them does not make them merely private and subjective any more than seeing and hearing a plane fly overhead makes the phenomenon of the plane a purely private and not a public phenomenal object—though of course the physical plane has a different kind of objective status.

So we may say that interpreting music is interpreting a common and public phenomenal object, about which we can talk intelligibly to one another: and learning to know and understand music is a development of objective knowledge.

A perceptive interpretation (or a 'good understanding') of a piece of music can only be achieved in a perceptive experience of the music itself. This generalization goes, I think, for all the arts, including literature. Direct study of the works themselves, and the discriminating enjoyment of them, is essential. But interpretation of literature, in contrast to pure music, is affected by its special conditions, not present in discussions of pure music. One is that as a representative art, literature has a subject matter, 'life', distinguishable from the art of literature itself. How does the author interpret his subject matter, 'life'? (How is the character of Hamlet interpreted?) Another is that literature itself is language-using. Because of this, there is an overlap of the literary art medium, words, and words used in literary interpretation. This does not occur with pure music. Critical comments on works both of music and literature are, of course expressed in ordinary language. And such commentaries, in both fields, can quite sensibly be called, and are called, 'interpretative'. So far, so good. But literary criticism is in itself a huge 'literature', of different kinds, and, as developed during this century, a bewilderingly complex and technical one. René Wellek,[7] writing in the early 1960s, speaks of the many attempts to obliterate the distinctions between 'literary theory', 'the study of the principles of literature, its categories, criteria, and the like', 'literary criticism' (as directed on the works themselves), and 'literary history'. What he thinks (and I too think) to be the central focus of criticism, and the essential condition of interpretation, the holistic attention to, and absorption in, is the concrete works themselves. This is, in literature, in danger of being squeezed out of existence by the enormous (some might say 'monstrous') growth of what is called 'literary theory and criticism'—structuralism, semiotics and the rest—claiming to be independent bodies of thought and knowledge existing in their own right. Wellek observes that more or less totalitarian claims have been made for some of these disciplines. Much of this debate is purely verbal: a further example of the incredible confusion of tongues, the veritable Tower of Babel which seems to be one of the most ominous features of our culture. He argues against Northrop Frye's attempt to erect literary theory into the uniquely worthwhile discipline and to expel criticism (in our sense of criticism of concrete works) from literary study. (Since the 1960s the Tower of Babel seems to have got higher!)

These controversies, fortunately, are beyond the scope of this book— and in any case I have neither the knowledge nor the competence to deal with them adequately. But it would have been difficult even to mention

interpretation in literature without at least alluding to them, and I hope
the relevance is clear.

5. Art and symbols

That we can interpret meaning in works of art only by imaginative,
holistic, intuitive entry into their phenomenal 'life' is to say that, in an
important sense, a work of art 'means itself'. I epitomize this by saying
that the meaning of a (phenomenal) work of art is 'meaning-embodied'.
But to say that the work 'means itself' sounds nonsensical if we use
'symbol' in some of its more usual senses. I have written a good deal
about this elsewhere:[8] but the use of the word 'symbol' relevantly to art is
so important that I must return to it briefly here.

No sense of 'symbol' as the word is used outside the discussion of art is
directly applicable to art. The commonest use, of ordinary language, as
'semiotic', will not do. Word-using imaginative literature does of course
employ semiotic symbols referring directly to ideas or conceptions, and
indirectly through these, to their objective uses, but of course in their
fictional contexts. And in the fictional contexts of literary works of art the
correspondence of words with their referential meanings is assimilated
artistically into the single artistic meaning of the whole work in a way
which is quite different from the way in which the referential meaning of
words is assimilated logically in a systematic logical statement or
argument. The work of art is not a 'symbolic system' in the sense in
which a discursive argument is a logical system in which the particular
meanings of the words must be consistently held to throughout the
argument. The 'meaning' of any particular part of a work of art is not
predeterminately fixed but is only fully artistically understood through
its organic relation to the whole. It is the art-work as a whole which is
'the' symbol. The ordinary semiotic symbol can, up to a point, be
detached, and used elsewhere. The aesthetically meaning words of a
poem cannot be so detached.

Another sense of symbol which has played some part in recent
discussions of art is the *iconic*, where the symbol is similar to, or
resembles, its object. This hardly needs consideration here since, by
implication, it has already been ruled out. The trees in Constable's
paintings are not simply *like* real trees. Cézanne's *Mont Sainte Victoire* is
not simply like the real thing. An iconic view of symbolism leaves out the
artists' interpretation of their subject, how they see it, value it, and leaves

out the limitations and potentialities of the medium. The same applies, *mutatis mutandis*, to other arts.

I will only mention the Freudian account of the symbol in relation to art, and shall not discuss it, as it seems to me to be strongly reductive in ways we should have to reject. Jung, though terribly vague and inclined to use the same words with different meanings inconsistently (the artist in him perhaps dominating his duty to discursive logic!), has far deeper insights into art. But he too in the end is reductive. Very generally for Jung, a symbol is the very best expression of what we cannot know or say otherwise than through the symbol. The Cross, for instance, symbolizes vast complexities of meanings, which cannot only *not* all be said adequately in words, but which have profound affective implications. In a way it is an intentional symbol and one might be deceived into thinking it as, nearly, a very simple work of art. Like art, it seems to gather into itself a complex and unsayable collocation of meanings. But any cross is still a *general* symbol: *any* cross will do. It is not an individual, as a work of art is. And Jung's own interpretation of the symbol precludes it from being art, for he still thinks of the symbol as ultimately referential. The meaning is not, in our experience of it, really and truly gathered into and transformed in the symbol, as it must be in art. The meaning is not truly embodied in what we see, as we see it. Rather it *stands for* a cluster of partly ineffable meanings beyond the symbol. If we gaze at a cross, we do not gaze at the detailed physical form, or with the same kind of attention as we would gaze at the detailed physical form of Rembrandt's *Prodigal Son*. There, certainly, we think far beyond the physical presentation to its parabolic meanings. But it is the *way* in which Rembrandt expresses, in the strokes and forms of his drawings, his understanding and his feelings for these meanings, so precious and significant for him as a man, which count in our absorption with the picture itself.

Since none of these other senses of 'symbol' are adequate to art, we come back to the unique 'embodiment-symbol', where meaning is so inseparable from the thing we see or hear or read (as we hear or see or read it) that it is incomprehensible and unsayable in other ways. We apprehend the symbolic meaning of the work which is the symbol by attending to the form of the symbol itself.

If this is so, it displaces the idea of art as an 'expression' from the central position it has occupied in so much writing about the arts since the eighteenth century. It would be absurd to deny that expression and expressiveness of several different kinds is involved in the initiation of art, the process of making it, and in the final product. ('Expression', I am assuming, is commonly thought of as 'expression of emotions', sometimes of 'feeling and emotions' but often without discriminating between these. Since, as I have argued, 'feeling' is the wider notion, in these remarks I shall here say 'feeling'.)

One accepts, then, that there is no harm in saying that expression of 'feelings' is involved in the initiation, processes of making, and enjoyment of art, so long as it is realized that feelings are cognitive as well as affective, that art expresses ideas and feelings of, and for, ideas and things; and that feelings are for, and of, values.

Any story of the initiation and process of art-making, as well as the enjoyment of given works, must recognize that the expression of feelings *can* occur in a number of senses and ways. The initiation of a work may be set off by a very personal feeling in the artist, which he/she wants to 'express'. Milton's anger, for instance, is expressed in 'Avenge, O Lord thy slaughtered saints ...' Mozart wants to 'express' his love in a symphony. Bach 'expresses' his deeply religious feelings in his *Passions*. Constable expresses his love of natural scenery, Picasso, his horror, in *Guernica*. Stravinsky (though for his own reasons he denied it) expressed his feelings in the ballet scores for *The Fire Bird* or *The Rite of Spring*. At the other end, the receiving end, we naturally speak of the infinitely various 'expressiveness' of colours, contours, volumes in visual arts, of the various forms in music, of the arrangement of words in poetry, gestural posture and movements in dance. And in the middle, the actual creative process itself, it would be perverse to deny that the artist feels himself/herself as 'expressing'—*something*. But what?

The baffling, and quite extraordinary, difficulty about the use of the words 'expression' and 'expressive' as applied to art (and it is doubtful whether there will ever be an agreed solution) is that the verb 'to express' is naturally transitive: if I express, I must be expressing *something*. In the use of 'express' in ordinary speech, there is some general concept or set of concepts which can be expressed in variously different forms of words, and in different languages. If a new society is being formed, for instance, its aims can be expressed satisfactorily and equally well in various forms and arrangements of words. And if the word 'embody' is used here instead of 'expression', it is simply as a synonym for 'expression'. But 'expression' in art is just not like this. If art is called 'expressive', what is meant is not that this art is merely one form of expressing a clear general idea or system of ideas among other forms which might equally well express the same identical idea. Although the arts grow out of life, are continuous with life, are a form of living, and, in the senses illustrated above, do express life-feelings, it is true also that imaginative art transcends life in creating something new, unique and individual, an emergent, and cannot be reduced back to life outside art. And the new 'something' which art creates, *what* it creates, is the individual structured work of art itself in which is embodied, inseparably from its construction in its medium, its irreducibly artistic meaning. If we say 'expression', it must be conceived reflexively. It is for this reason that I so stress meaning-*embodied*. This meaning cannot be *told* (apart from the way in which it is 'told' in and by the work), in any other way by any description using general words: it can and must be known directly, intuitively, in experience of it.

So, if the word 'expression' is to be used as applying strictly within the unique category of art, it can only properly be taken as intending that the meaning which the art 'expresses' is to be found in the actual work itself as we experience it with understanding. The word 'express' must be understood reflexively. And since the transitiveness (to some other 'meaning') of the words 'express' and 'expression' is so endemic to its ordinary use, it seems better, in strict philosophical use, to say '(artistic) embodiment' rather than 'expression'. This does not cut out its looser uses, which can very rightly suggest art's organic relations with 'real life'. I have no objection to the convenient use of 'expressive arts' as a general category. But 'embodiment' suggests the categorical difference between the conceptions of 'art' as a sort of self-contained monad and of 'life' outside it.*

---

* Of a recent contemporary half-baked claim that works of art have 'no meaning', and 'refer only to themselves', one might say that the statement really is '*half*-baked'.

Chapter VI
Understanding Persons

It has already been shown that the meanings of the words 'knowledge' and 'understanding' must vary with what it is that we are trying to know and understand—say facts or values discursively understood, or works of art aesthetically understood. Different kinds of understanding involve different stresses and emphases—on intellect, knowledge-about, feeling, direct acquaintance and intuition, personal involvement. In the understanding and knowledge of and between persons—perhaps more complex than any other—in the adequacy and truth of our apprehensions we should expect all these to be included, and, very much so, our own personal involvements. But more: in the understanding of other persons (as well as ourselves) an important *moral* factor is involved. Persons and personal relations are at the heart of morality; 'respect for persons' a very generally accepted central principle of morality. So understanding of the qualities and values of moral character in the would-be understander of other persons will be a condition of personal understanding in any depth. An incorrigible egotist, for example, is self-debarred from more than superficial understanding of other people. On the other hand, some of the outgoing agape, in which there is a fusion of some sympathy and warmth with detached objectivity, may be found to be a positive qualification for personal understanding. To the degree in which it is attained, deep understanding of other persons may be something of a moral achievement. So, generally speaking, the conceptual understanding of interpersonal relations has, as well as a psychological and epistemological interest, a moral as well as an epistemological factor. After some preliminaries (and in Chapter VII) we shall return to this vitally important aspect of the human person and character.

1. Personal involvement and detachment in the knowledge of persons

Although all human knowledge is personal in the sense of being a possession of personal mind, much of it, we know, is relatively impersonal. Polanyi, in the Part of his *Personal Knowledge* significantly entitled 'Knowing and being', shows how, as we ascend in the scale of being, the participation of the knower becomes more and more important.

> Facts about living things are more highly personal than the facts of the inanimate world. Moreover, as we ascend to higher manifestations of life, we have to exercise ever more personal faculties—involving a more far-reaching participation of the knower—in order to understand life. For whether an organism operates more as a machine or more by a process of equipotential integration, our knowledge of its achievements must rely on a comprehensive appreciation of it which cannot be specified in terms of more impersonal facts, and the logical gap between our comprehension and the specification of our comprehension goes on deepening as we ascend the evolutionary ladder . . . As we proceed to survey the ascending stages of life, our subject matter will tend to include more and more of the very faculties on which we rely for understanding it.[1]

This is greatest of all in man's knowledge of man.

In what are called 'the Human Sciences', psychology and sociology, studies of persons and persons in relation, the methods of observation, empirical generalization, conceptual thinking, are in standard employment, and up to a point legitimately so. But when we are thinking of the understanding of persons who are, though particular, also individual in a very special sense, the words 'observation', 'generalization', 'conceptual', though in some contexts legitimate, can be misleading, and certainly limiting. Sometimes we may coolly observe another person. At other times an attitude of cool observation may destroy the conditions of personal understanding. Sometimes we may quite properly generalize: but can we generalize, say statistically, about individual persons, without thinking of persons as simply 'instances'? We cannot. And conceptual thinking about persons, being necessarily abstract, can get in the way of, or even destroy, direct understanding of *this* person. I am certainly not ruling out these approaches to the understanding of persons, but am merely pointing out the dangers of the exclusive use of some of these approaches. Into the mature synoptic understandings which one person may have of another, many modes of thinking and feeling may have to be assimilated and fused together to give illuminated insight.

2. Factors and approaches in understanding persons—scientific and other

A person to be understood can, in one context, or aspect, be an epistemological 'object'—but different from a mere thing, a purely material object, scientific object, or art object. The person as 'object' is a natural psychophysical organism, with a heredity, subject to environmental and cultural influences, is a particular and individual person with a personal history, all of which affect and to a large extent determine what he/she now is, his/her 'make-up'. The embodied person also has personal and private experiences—sensations, feelings, emotions—he/she has opinions, beliefs, sentiments, a certain outlook on life, active tendencies, habits, intentions, and so on. And he/she is also in some sense 'free'. Of the person who 'observes' the other person, the same things generally are true.

When one person is ordinarily trying to understand another, a new factor enters. The personal 'object' of understanding *responds*, or can respond, to another person trying to understand him/her. He/she might of course not want to be 'understood'; might shut up like a clam. This, however, would be one kind of response. But in any case, his/her free positive responses become part of the data to be understood—and his/her responses are an ongoing continuous factor.

So far the picture has been assumed to be limited to that of two people, one trying to understand, the other responding in some way, which includes some at least minimal attempt of the subject to understand the 'understander' and what he/she is getting at. But this situation, though it is important, is only one of a number of possible relationships between persons who want to understand other persons.

There is the pure scientific approach, 'objective' in that what is studied are objects belonging to the public world, and behaviour which can be objectively assessed—as distinct from the subjective states behind them which may be expressed in the behaviour. There can also, on this view, be inferences and psychological theories about subjective states, important in their own way. But, on such interpretation of 'scientific', it is overt public behaviour which is the proper object of study. 'Responses' here mean, presumably, behaviour.

Psychological studies divide themselves broadly into two types. One is the psychology which claims to be scientific and general, classifying people statistically according to general categories—involving psychometry, scoring of tests, rating behaviour, probability frequencies, and so on. The other presupposes acquaintance of person with person and is concerned with individual understanding. Qua psychological a good deal of it can be called clinical, from the perhaps rather distant and relatively impersonal stance of some psychiatrists towards their patients, to the closer touch other psychotherapists or psychological social workers have in relation to those with whom they are dealing. Then there is the whole very wide range of contacts between ordinary people, not acting as scientists or psychologists or healers, but in day-to-day personal encounters of every kind and quality, including, at one end, very close personal relationships.

Human persons behave publicly, certainly; but one cannot possibly understand that behaviour without attending to and considering as important the subjective factors, including feelings, emotions, motives, intentions, of which the behaviour is an expression, and of the inner personal history which shapes sentiments and attitudes. This inner personal story cannot be understood by employing only the deliberately self-limiting methods of natural science which so manifestly succeeds by focusing on certain selected aspects of the objective world, and excluding everything else. Persons are subjects: and understanding of persons can never get far by ignoring essential subjective data, as a strict behaviouristic approach must do.

Radical behaviourism apart, there are other familiar brands of psychology which insist on being counted 'scientific'. They do not, in theory, deny or entirely ignore the existence of inner individual personal life, but they sit loose to it or shy away from it, from the direct perceptively open approach to other persons. Their method is to come to individual persons (when they do) with already formed generalizations, testing to see whether individuals conform to or vary from certain hypothetically given, already formed, psychological categories. Certainly one cannot come to any understanding of anything without an already formed conceptual background. But general categories, though indispensable and up to a point helpful, can gain one sort of insight at the expense of another. They can be obstacles to individual understanding if they are allowed to dominate entirely the approach to individual persons. There must be a certain suspension, and an openness. The meshed grills of conceptual screens *can* artificially atomize what is flux and unity.

The strictly categorial approach in psychology can give us information and increase our understanding of human nature. Questionnaires, based on certain assumptions, or personality profiles, can tell us quite a lot about individuals. Again, vocational tests used in guidance have their uses—though they are controlled by the nature of job analysis or vocational demands, and cannot (and do not pretend to) cover the indefinitely wide ranges of vocational capacities. And personality profiles are not only limited by the generality and limited number of the categories they assume, but by unavoidable differences of comprehension and interpretation of the given questions on the part of those who are being examined, depending on their individual personal backgrounds, including their relations to other people.

Statistical methods, consideration of probabilities, the classification of test scores, ratings, etc., have their general importance too as well as their limitations, for general educational and sociological research. They are not directly relevant, since these methods are concerned with putting individuals into classes, and not with personal understanding.

Another brand of psychology, presupposing some personal acquaintance between two people, includes the 'clinical' approach already alluded to. The word derives from 'bedside' and suggests a detachment of doctor from patient which *sometimes* can prevail when, say, a psychiatrist behind a desk is questioning a patient in a detached impersonal way. But always, because we are here thinking of face-to-face situations, there are at least minimal personal relations between doctor and patient (or even 'client'). This is not incompatible with their also being 'impersonal'.

With such wide variations, it is impossible to make one simple generalization about the degree and kind of understanding which can be achieved in these kinds of situation. The competent and sensitive psychiatric social worker, and some psychotherapists, may understand aspects of individual patients which the psychiatric specialist does not, their involvements with the patient being different. But one condition, and it is a formal limitation, is that all these operations and relations have a practical end, namely therapy. They do, by their very definition, fall short of full personal relationships. 'Patients' are, in the nature of things, 'subject-objects' to be helped in some way if possible.

3. Moral understanding

So far, with some observations about the presence (and absence) of personal involvement in the understanding of other persons, our approach has been mainly a brief review of some psychological approaches to the understanding of other minds. Note now a change of emphasis—from 'minds' to 'persons'. Minds are the minds of persons; it is persons who have minds; 'person' is thus the broader, inclusive term. Understanding of a person in any depth includes the understanding of how his/her mind works; but the understanding of that entails considerations which go far beyond the person's individual psychology into moral questions.

A person is, essentially, a self-conscious being, able to be aware of his/her thoughts, feelings, emotions, desires, actions, purposes, to reflect on the nature of his/her own life. To be able to ask questions— sometimes very ultimate questions—about oneself and one's life is part of the definition of a person. This capacity is not simply contingent; it is of the essence of personhood. For it is not through possessing a fixed 'nature', from which thoughts, feelings, actions logically flow, that a person is a person. Personhood, personality, is a flowing development of, and from, self-reflections, questionings, judgements. This of course in no way denies the conditioning influences of heredity and environment: but personhood is an emergent from them.

Another way of saying much the same thing is to recognize that a key to understanding any person is to know what they value, and whether their values are 'true', or 'pseudo' or 'false'. There are two (connected) levels of question, or concept, here. We may be said to 'value' something if we are 'interested' in it positively or negatively, desire it or reject it. (We can ignore negative values here.) Thus heroin is in this sense a 'value' to addicts, a positive value to the addict-at-the-time. But we know that 'values' in this sense are 'subjective', are, on a longer view, *dis*values. The same general use of the word 'value' holds—unless one is a sceptic about the objectivity of values—of other classes of value, for example, artistic or moral. How objectivity is tested is of course another, and controversial, question. We made some comments in the last chapter on the objectivity of artistic values: in the next chapter (section 7) we shall look at moral values.

But if we assume without lengthy argument any 'existentialist' view which says that we *create* values by choosing or deciding what is to *count* as value, then our understanding of another person will be limited to a purely naturalistic account of that person. We may discover that he/she likes adventure, or security, values respectability and prestigious motor cars, believes in freedom and democracy or in Fascism, admires self-assertive and ruthless power, or temperance, benevolence, love, freedom or authoritarian discipline, justice, courage ... But we shall not, logically, on the assumption that what counts as value is created simply by preferences, likings, desires, be able to make any moral *judgements* on these. In fact, we shall be unable to avoid making some 'judgements'. This will, however, be inconsistent with the basic existentialist assumption, and be without rational basis, because the only ground of such 'judgement' can be one's own individual preferences or likings. Even if one believes that one ought not to make moral judgements on others because they must be left free to create their own 'moral' values, the belief has no rational ground, but is a matter of one's own personal feelings.

This is an impossible position. Moral values arise and have their meaning in the context of the life of persons. Ideally speaking, it is only within the full context of personal and interpersonal life and of the values that arise therein that the character of any person (including of course oneself) can be understood. However unattainable this understanding is in full, to accept finally and be satisfied with morally unjudging, naturalistic description of a person is to submit to a truncated view of personal understanding.

4. Personal relationships: reciprocity

In this section, the 'understanding of persons' is taken to be the understanding between particular and individual persons, in some depth—sometimes on one side, sometimes on the other, sometimes mutual. Because it is understanding in this sort of dimension, special problems of communication in 'public' language can arise. The aim, as in all understanding, is 'objective', to achieve as far as possible 'true knowledge', and here what may be called with particular appropriateness, 'holistic insight'. Into this seeking for knowledge and understanding, subjective elements inevitably enter. Personal limitations, one's past history, particular experiences, one's biases, prejudices, idiosyncracies, are always to some degree involved. This is of course true of any kind of understanding. But subjective limitations on one side or the other, or both, are more easily offset and checked where the object of investigation is the structure of 'things'. There we have the safeguards, via a carefully monitored common language, of the systematic findings of others. But if personal, subjective, possibly emotional, factors are part of, internal to, the very process of understanding others, the 'objectivity' must be of a specially qualified kind, perhaps something of an achievement. The last sentence in the earlier quotation from Polanyi is apposite. 'As we proceed to survey the ascending stages of life, our subject matter will tend to include more and more of the very faculties on which we rely for understanding it.'

In human beings there are the observable features to be taken account of in understanding them. But 'observe', as we have said, tends to have a limited connotation, to what, more or less, can be noted down as the behaviourist would record it.

In human beings there are not only the 'observable features': there are the expressive looks and actions, motivated gestures, varying according to circumstances and in particular in relation to the other person being met. We apprehend their meaningfulness directly, and not by 'inferences' from 'behaviour'. And generally, there is the important factor of reciprocity, and what Martin Buber[2] called the 'I-Thou' relationship. If I meet someone, not in some role as, say, a scientist or a doctor, but directly face to face as another person, I do not simply *observe*, impersonally, their features and expressive demeanour, as implying 'shy', 'hostile', 'forbidding' . . . or 'friendly', 'warm', inviting exchange. I, my attitude, feelings, responses, are immediately and spontaneously affected, and so is the progress (or otherwise) of our relationship. If the other person is shy or hostile, our relationships tend to be inhibited, at least for a time: if they are friendly and warm, we may get to know one another quite quickly. Of course it is far more complex than that. A person can seem shy or hostile and yet be, underneath, interested and anxious to make contact; or their friendliness may turn out to be superficial. And the same goes for me. But the point is that in reciprocal relationships the kind of understanding which develops depends generally on an 'I-Thou' or person-to-person relationship, which tends to influence its particular structural features.

Some of the relationships involved in the understanding of persons are reciprocal; some, as we have said, are obviously not—for example, the clinical role of the professional doctor or psychiatrist.

Dr Frances Berenson, in her valuable book, *Understanding Persons*, places a central emphasis on reciprocity of personal relationships as a condition of deep and full interpersonal understanding. 'It is only in reciprocal personal relationships that subjective aspects of a person's life have a chance of spontaneously and fully manifesting themselves. Attitudes and reciprocal responses are of crucial importance—these are lacking in the case of scientific knowledge.'[3] Understanding at this level is what she calls a 'creative process'. Such personal relationships involve a measure of sustained outgoingness and spontaneity both of approach and response. There must be a mutual feeling of confidence on the basis of which reciprocity can take place. Affinity, too, is required, both in a general sense in which there is a necessity for affinity between the knower and the knowable, with response and counter-response in turn, and in a particular sense, which can only be spelled out in detail with reference to particular cases.[4] Again, she argues, *emotional* involvement is required as a spur to interest in the other person. 'Caring about, being involved, having certain emotionally charged attitudes towards certain activities, responses and the like, is what makes possible the exercise and engagement in those activities, what decides the kind of engagement in them'.[5] And not only this: emotional involvement can clarify understanding. In seeing and feeling the reactions and responses of others in given situations, 'the power which provokes real understanding here is the emotional power which illuminates and reveals to our understanding what may otherwise remain hidden'.[6]

These claims I think need some scrutiny. The claim that a high degree of reciprocity is a necessary condition of deep understanding, is open to question—unless indeed it were only reciprocal understanding that one was considering. While I have insisted, as she does, that the purely scientific approach is inadequate for personal understanding, and that the affectively sterilized attitudes of some 'clinical' approaches can limit understanding, the reaction against non-reciprocal understanding can be too strong. I think that in the relationship between persons in *asymmetrical* relationship, there can be a great deal of profound understanding.

The range of these possible asymmetrical personal relationships is quite wide. In a chapter of my book *Ways of Knowledge and Experience*,[7] 'Variations of personal relationships', I referred generally to some of these. After pointing out that human relationships may vary with degrees of intimacy, with the social situations in which they occur, and after affirming that emotional conditions may vary very greatly and may affect the quality and degree of interpersonal knowledge, I went on to discuss the *symmetry* and the *asymmetry* of relationships. Here one must distinguish between what may be called symmetry or asymmetry of *status*, and symmetry or asymmetry in the reciprocity of *response*. Status, in any particular situation at one particular time, is something given, and formal. Reciprocity, symmetrical or asymmetrical, is a dynamic concept, and can vary within the given and formal status relationship. Examples of status difference would be adult (say, parent or teacher) and child, doctor and patient, employer and employed. Difference in social status would be another example. Obviously the categories may overlap. Within any of these status situations, the dynamics of reciprocal response may vary greatly, as we have seen. Adult—parents, teachers and others—may be on easy terms with children and children with adults:

or adults may be ill at ease with children or may 'talk down' to them. Similarly with employer and employed. And so on.

5. Emotion, feeling, and personal understanding

These are all situations in which what would generally be called 'emotional' factors are involved. That is if we take 'emotional' in a broad sense, including emotional dispositions, and do not think only of extreme examples of occurrent emotions by which we are 'rocked'. Into every human relationship, even when acting in a *role* (for example, as teacher or professional adviser), we come with dispositional emotional attitudes, and very often, if not always, with prejudices. They are part of our make-up. We are naturally, and very often irrationally, attracted or repelled by people we see or meet. Political, social, moral, religious . . . emotional dispositions do colour at least our first reactions to other people. We are emotionally biased one way or the other, and this tends to open or close our minds towards better understanding. And as the dispositions are powerful, built up through time and the cumulative effect of highly emotional feelings in the past, it may be difficult indeed, when questions of understanding are involved, for even rationally disposed people to overcome them.

So if we speak of 'emotional involvement' we must distinguish in this connection between 'right' and 'wrong' emotional involvements, 'right' and 'wrong' here meaning those which make for better understanding and those which work against it. The 'right' or beneficial involvements emanate from dispositions which can be cultivated and educated, a morally normative process. Among such emotional dispositions to be cultivated are included what are sometimes described as sentiments for truth and objectivity, and along with these the disposition to respect and care about other human beings as persons, irrespective of whether they are 'attractive' or 'unattractive', lovable or hateful. If dispositions such as these latter are in active operation, they would be most favourable conditions for the understanding of others.

It is often said that 'love' is a condition making for the understanding of others. But though it is true, for example, that sexual love keeps two people interested in one another (for as long as it lasts), it does not in the least follow that they really understand one another. Sometimes, they do; but this is contingent on other factors, intelligence, for instance. Natural sexual love is certainly emotionally biased in favour of the loved one: it can, notoriously, be 'blind' too. If love is to qualify as a highly favourable condition for insight into others, it must be of a different kind—or leavened by a different kind—the agape referred to in another context.

I was not then, and am not now, concerned with the theological or religious aspects of agape, whether, or how, something of the assumed divine agape can be infused into human beings. Whatever one thinks about that, it is a familiar fact of experience that some persons at least are possessed of, and can and do cultivate and express concern for other human beings whatever their peculiarities, their likeability or dislikeability, their virtues or their vices, and can look at them with some objectivity. Such dispositions can be cultivated, and educated. It is important that they should be. This in no way excludes the presence of eros too, the natural attraction of one person to another, often, but not necessarily, sexual. Where agapistic sentiment is present it can (and should, if understanding is sought) leaven and transform 'erotic' emotions where such are also present.

But language which speaks in the context of understanding between persons, of 'emotional involvement', is of dubious value because of the ordinary associations of the term. In so far as the term does properly apply, the 'emotional involvement' will probably include an agapistic disposition which, as operative, is directed towards the other person. There is what one might call 'agapistic objectivity' of outlook, making for, or towards, an agapistically loving insight into the other. It is on one side a cognitive vision which can penetrate the more deeply because it is motivated by love in the agapistic sense. Human agape, in so far as it can be attained, is a general sentiment, or a general emotional disposition of caring towards human persons as such, which in principle (ideally) transcends natural bias and on its cognitive side makes for objective understanding.

It seems better, however, as it was in the case of art, to speak of 'feeling' rather than of 'emotion' or 'emotional involvement' as far as the cognitive side of personal understanding goes. When we speak of emotion and emotional involvement, a strong affective emphasis can overshadow or even blot out the recognition of the cognitive element in emotion. We can, and do, sensibly speak of 'feeling (cognitively) our way' towards finer discrimination. The cognitive feeling has affect which sensitively guides its cognitive explorations in understanding. This can be said of emotion too, but the stirring-up of sometimes very marked psycho-physical affect in emotions (which, we have said, are episodic rather than constantly present as feeling is) can make the use of the terms 'emotion' and 'emotional' misleading. We *can* speak of 'feeling our way'.

But it would be strange to say 'emotioning our way' though it would not necessarily be false! It will be agapistic *feeling* (dispositional or occurrent) which will chiefly or characteristically monitor perceptiveness in the understanding of others, rather than strong emotion. And if there are deep emotions sometimes, a joy in the growth of this perceptiveness may be part of its source. But a storm of emotion (even agapistic!) could distort vision. Agapistic feeling, having a warmth absent from the purely clinical approach, can temper and guide cognitiveness, and it can absorb and assimilate psychological understanding in a way which perhaps would be difficult with strong, perhaps overwhelming, emotion.

6. Reciprocity, symmetrical and asymmetrical

There can be no doubt of the importance of reciprocity in personal relationships. Where it subsists, the subjective aspects of a person's life can manifest themselves freely and develop, and are 'points of growth' for both persons. Generally speaking we *become*, from earliest youth, through our community with, and differences from, others. We come to understand ourselves better and more objectively as we could not understand ourselves at all in the absence of such interactions.

Ideally, as I have suggested, this takes place perhaps at its best between 'consenting' adults, and particularly between close friends, knowledgeably equipped with the relevant psychological understanding, with mutual sympathies, and with each possessing mature experience. Here the relationship will be, more or less, symmetrical.

But what about reciprocity where the relationship is asymmetrical? And may there not be deep understanding of other persons where, at least in the ordinary sense of the word, there is no reciprocity? It may be useful to look briefly at four types of such relationships. The first is clinical, the second educational, the third the relationship between novelists or dramatists and their created characters, and the fourth that between biographers and their subjects.

The first case is one where the *general* situation could be labelled '*clinical*', but where, within that situation, the psychological 'doctor' or the 'counsellor' has managed to establish a 'good', that is a sympathetic, warm, imaginative relationship with the other person, so that the other is relaxed and co-operative. Here, in a very asymmetrical situation, there is, on the one side, the attitude just described, an outgoing concern on the part of the 'doctor' or 'counsellor' for the other person, and a concern for the objective understanding of him/her. On the other side, there may or may not be responsiveness, but no particular concern for the person of the doctor or counsellor, or for the objective understanding of *him/her*. Nor, on this side, would there necessarily be the intellectual equipment or the technical knowledge required for such understanding. The 'emotional' relationship might be good, if asymmetrical, but the understanding would not be mutual or symmetrical. The 'patient' may learn a lot about himself/herself, but the patient's understanding of the 'doctor' may be very limited. We can therefore see the particular *kind* of importance this reciprocity may have.

The second case is the *educational* one, and particularly the asymmetrical relationship between teacher and pupil (where good personal relationships are quite crucial). Here one's estimation of such reciprocity as it is possible to achieve will depend on how important one thinks it is to consider and treat children (of all ages) in school as personal human beings. We have already rejected the idea that the scientific attitude is in itself adequate for the understanding of human persons. We would reject, *tout à fait*, views such as Thorndike's[8] at the beginning of the century, that a perfect and complete knowledge of human nature—a complete science of psychology—would tell the effect of every possible stimulus and the cause of every possible response in every possible human being. That is extreme, and dated: but not so dated as it may appear. I shall briefly refer to powerful American opinion in much the same category in Chapter VIII.

Teachers as such are not clinicians, even sympathetic ones; and pupils are not voluntary patients! Nor, if we suppose reciprocity of personal relationships important, can the conditions for it in these days—or indeed at any time—be considered as built into the classroom situation! In so far as it is possible, it has to be achieved, or won, often in face of seemingly insuperable difficulties, demanding conviction, faith, courage, character (and sometimes special personal gifts) on the part of the teacher.

Classroom situations, concretely speaking, are very particular and individual, varying infinitely. Children in classes are both individuals and subject to group and mass influences. The conditions under which reciprocity of relationships can operate vary accordingly and in many ways. Apart from some general maxims about what used to be called 'class management', it is impossible to lay down any fixed rules about what a teacher ought to do in what are always *this* or *that* set of particular circumstances. What a teacher requires, almost above everything else, is what William Walsh once called 'tact', sense of 'touch'. Nevertheless, the good teacher's belief, faith, conviction, that children are individual persons, developing individually, not units to be manipulated and conditioned according to his/her own ideas, is crucial to everything he/she does in all these very particular circumstances, and it is infused into his/her intuitions. So that anything which can usefully be said can be said only at the level of general principles and ideals. The teacher's 'agapistic' self-discipline is called out and tested. What are usually called 'emotional' relationships with individuals have their familiar dangers. If 'emotion' is the right word it must be the 'right' emotion, agapistically leavened. More generally, the agapistic factor serves to offset the dangers of asymmetry which in itself can be an obstacle to reciprocity, and can engender 'talking down'. The older person *is* older, *is* (I am supposing) in authority, does know more, than the younger. And yet the address as between the older and the younger, if it is from person to person, can, in spite of the asymmetry, be reciprocal. Again and again one hears it said how memorable as high points of personal development such reciprocal encounters have been, not only as important 'emotional' occasions, but as initiations of fresh development and new insights. A.S. Neill may, possibly, have underestimated the *formal* natural fact of asymmetry (as well as the need for the hard disciplines of learning). But the love he had for his pupils and the love they had for him, in a way shows how the formal fact can be transcended and transmuted by this very love into fruitful personal relationship, in the quality of which there is no 'inequality', but a person-to-person community.

Are there possibilities of understanding other persons where there is *no* reciprocity in the direct face-to-face sense in which we have so far been taking it—or at least if there is reciprocity, the understanding operating in very special ways? The cases I have in mind are those mentioned above as the third and fourth—the relationship between novelists or dramatists and their created characters, and that between biographers and their subjects.

7. Is reciprocity necessary? Novels, drama, and biography

Novels and drama. Berenson discusses, in her book, with examples, the relationships between novelists and their depicted characters. Could the relationship be called a 'reciprocal' one? Not quite, at any rate in the sense in which we have been using the word so far. It is true that artist-novelists in the process of creating their characters may find that as the characters develop and become alive they take 'legs' and may walk away from them, or towards them, or in a metaphorical sense 'answer back', and may even 'help' their authors reflexively to understand themselves better. But the 'reciprocity' is of a special and limited kind. Yet there can surely be no doubt that, 'reciprocal' or not, the understanding by authors of their characters can be profound indeed.

There is some parallel here with questions which the *reader* of a great novel (or spectator of a great drama) may ask himself. Does having become 'acquainted' with Anna Karenina, or Levin, or Dorothea and Casaubon in *Middlemarch* 'do' anything to me in the way it might have done had I met them reciprocally as real people in real life? Perhaps a little; but clearly it is not the same as the sort of influence on my person which another person intimately known in real life could be. Yet of the possible enlargement of sympathies and understanding, and, I think, modification of one's own attitudes and perhaps behaviour, there is I believe little doubt. It does not necessarily happen: it depends on oneself and one's experiences. But speaking personally I believe, or at any rate like to feel, that after first reading Winifred Holt's *South Riding* my sympathetic understanding of sometimes deceitful and even vicious people, or of odiously calculating, or religiose, or sexually exploiting, or just foolish characters, had been greatly extended. The courageous ambivalence and self-contradictoriness of one chief character, the schoolmistress, I found lovable: and I *think* my sympathy with and understanding of real people developed a little!

None of it is the *same* as the reciprocal meeting of people in real life, the full quality of which, it is agreed, cannot be said in general statements. The literary artist, however, uses words and images perspicaciously, and we in our turn respond holistically. He/she is both objective and intuitively understanding of feelings, emotions, motives, and presents their workings in the detailed context of individual personal lives. There is here at least a very close analogy with what one comes to know and understand in reciprocal personal relations; and it is a major mode of personal understanding, yet with differences.

Then there is *biography*. In written biography there is no necessarily reciprocal relationship between either the writer and the subject, or between the reader and the subject depicted. As far as the writer is concerned, there are two different cases. One is where the writer *has been* in reciprocal relationship with the subject: the other is when he/she has not. Examples of the first would be Mrs Gaskell and Charlotte Brontë, or Quentin Bell and Virginia Woolf. In the second group would be Lynne Reid Banks' biography of Charlotte, and her account of the Brontë family, *Dark Quartet*. Or Robert Gittings' biography of Thomas Hardy. In the first case Mrs Gaskell and Charlotte knew one another well; and Quentin Bell had close reciprocal relations with Virginia and Vanessa, his aunts, and with his father Clive, as well as with Roger Fry and many others who appear in his book. His writing is based on this. But with him *as the writer of the book*, and the characters as depicted in the book, there is, of course, no direct ongoing reciprocal relationship. The biography is written, and comes from the author, about his subjects, and there is, now, no 'answering back'. In Quentin Bell's case, the writing is greatly enlivened and enriched by his personal contacts with all the people he writes about, and his artistic sensitivity as a writer brings it out. But the book has also a remarkable quality of psychical distance, a kind of objectivity about his father (whom he sees realistically) and the others of whom he writes. It is objective, but its objectivity is leavened by a sensitive understanding derived from his personal knowledge. The reader's understanding of the persons in the biography undoubtedly grows with the reading, and depends too on the building up of biographical detail, and of the implications of all the little contingencies which often, quite fortuitously, it seems, go to shape a life and a person. The reader's real understanding does grow. But none of it is reciprocal.

Biographers in the second group have never been in reciprocal relationship with their subjects. They have to rely on long and patient research, building up the factual background so as to show how the persons developed in personal reactions to it, were modified by, and in turn modified, contingent circumstances—all of this conditioned and made possible by the author's sympathetic and empathic imagination. The reader reads, comes to understand the persons so depicted, and, when the biography is notably good, comes to understand a great deal more than that. Until I had read *Dark Quartet* and its sequel I had not only no idea of the depth and strength and the quality of courage of Charlotte's fight against almost unbearable adversity. I also had no idea of how much her originality of mind and character revealed the desperate plight of women in her day, or of her genius as a first pioneer of women's rights. No reciprocity: but the reader *understands*.

8. Validation?

One question remains. How do we know—or can we know—that we have, at least in some degree, understood another person? In mathematics there is proof, in the natural sciences support from conceptual and empirical testing, positive or negative, in the arts a good deal of support from the build-up, through time, of sensitive and informed critical judgements. But, except in mathematics, no proof or finally incorrigible validation. Nor in the matter of understanding persons is there proof or final validation. At the scientific-psychological level there could be partial empirical verification. And there are validatory tests—conceptual coherence and comprehensiveness; and practical tests in the cumulative substantiation of our faith and trust in a person, or as shown in our ability to 'deal' with him/her—a pragmatic confirmation. But of the imaginative, projective, indwelling insight which is an essential feature of interpersonal understanding there can only be qualified assurance. Much of it cannot be 'said'; and it could be wrong. In conclusion of this chapter I will quote Polanyi,[9] whose understanding of the range and depth of personal knowledge is in our time unrivalled:

> A personal knowledge accepted by indwelling may appear merely subjective. It cannot be fully defended here against this suspicion. But we can already distinguish between the accrediting of an articulate framework, be it a theory, a religious ritual or a work of art, and the accrediting of an experience, whether within such a framework or as a visionary contemplation. It might appear questionable whether there can be anything to accredit where nothing seems to be asserted. We see what we see, we smell what we smell and we feel what we feel, and there seems no more to it. Experiences that make no claim whatever would be truly incorrigible. But we must allow in the first place for the fact that what we see or feel depends very much on the way we make sense of it, and in this respect it is corrigible . . . Any deliberate existential use of the mind may be said to succeed or fail in achieving a desired experience . . . Experiences can be compared in *depth*, and the more deeply they affect us, the more *genuine* they may be said to be . . .
>
> The acceptance of different kinds of articulate systems as mental dwelling places is arrived at by a process of gradual appreciation, and all these acceptances depend to some extent on the content of relevant experiences: but the bearing of natural science on facts of experience is much more specific than that of mathematics, religion or the various arts . . .
>
> Our personal participation is in general greater in a validation than in a verification. The emotional coefficient of assertion is intensified as we pass from the sciences to the neighbouring domains of thought. But both *verification* and *validation* are everywhere an acknowledgement of a commitment: they claim the presence of something real and external to the speaker. As distinct from both of these, *subjective* experiences can only be said to be *authentic*, and authenticity does not involve a commitment in the sense in which both verification and validation do.

VII
Moral Understanding and Moral Action

1. The isolation of reason in moral thinking

Professional philosophical ethics tends to reflect powerfully in its account of the moral life, the image of its own form and the habits of thinking it cultivates, analytic-synthetic logical thinking. This is not surprising and it is up to a point inevitable. As in pure mathematics and in empirical and theoretic sciences the effects of the forms, habits and conventions of mathematical and scientific thinking are stamped upon their subjects, as is the influence of the tests they use to check their truth, so one might expect it to be in ethics. But the comparison can be misleading. Mathematics and science are ruled by logic and other impersonal criteria of truth. Moral philosophy—or at any rate some forms of it—strives hard over its more debatable kind of objectivity, but in a field, the field of human persons in relation, the understanding makes demands which cannot be achieved simply by logical and empirical thinking in the sense in which science is empirical. If ethics is concerned, as it is, with persons and persons' lives, and is 'short' on its understanding of human action, its particularities and the concrete complexities within human persons, it will be 'short' on its understanding of morality. And it *is* apt to be 'short': a good deal of the philosophy of morals *is* apt to impose the one-sided analytic and separative conceptual habits of the discipline of ethics upon its ideas of what moral persons are and what practical moral actions ought to be. Particularly it is prone to the pervasive habit of separating feeling from thinking, reason and reasoning from moral sentiments, 'will' from thinking and feeling, and theoretical knowledge from the knowledge of direct experience. And in the separation reason is made the dominating factor over all else. This is absurd. It is not that, on any viable account, ratiocination is denied its unchallengeable part in all moral thinking and doing. What is wrong is that the reason here should be thought to function as a faculty separate from all else, from feeling and will. In fact and in effect this is what virtually happens in certain kinds of thinking about morals. I say 'in effect' and 'virtually' because philosophers who think in this way are too sophisticated nowadays not to acknowledge feeling, sentiment, motive, will. But the tendency is to think of these as additional factors operating independently. There must be, of course, different *emphases* at different times on thinking, reasoning, feeling, deciding, acting. But all are internally related, as the parts of a single organism. It is the person who reasons, feels, decides, acts. It is easy to overlook this obvious fact.

When one is reflecting on persons and morality, it is necessary to be analytic, as it is necessary too to synthesize the concepts analysed-out into an as-far-as-possible coherent system. But further than this, it is necessary continually to be testing theory against actual and particular moral experience of the ordinary persons who are subjects and agents in moral experience. These are prior and directly given. Fictions in moral philosophy are necessary as a stage of it. But in themselves they are abstractions, and if one stays long in the rarefied atmosphere of philosophy, there is great danger of manipulating fictions in substitute for reflection on concrete factual experience.

Kant in some of his moral thinking is a familiar and often-quoted example of this. 'Persons' are to be respected. But they are not conceived as the persons we meet daily, but as (ideal) 'rational beings', all the same qua rational, without consideration of concrete differences of personality and particular circumstances. Such persons 'give' and are determined by 'law universal' and (in Kant) their 'love' for other persons is coldly 'practical' because coldly 'rational'—not the 'pathological' love I might have for you in sympathy *because* you are living in distressful circumstances (an empirical matter).

Again utilitarianism, though the polar opposite of Kantian ethics in its emphasis on experience, makes, both in its 'rule' and its 'act' forms, a *calculus* central to its theory. There are several effects of this. If the calculus is an 'ideal', it is an impossible one, a faulty conceptual fiction, for calculation of human happiness is impossible, and a confused idea. It is confused because even so far as we can predict the effects of our acts (and consideration of such effects is a part of moral obligation), all we can do is to promote the *conditions* of other people's happiness or other good. We cannot, strictly, one-sidedly *cause* another person's personal good. He/she, in his/her freedom, has to 'make' good out of the conditions offered. People without the basic necessities of life, or even without the luxuries, may be miserable and unhappy. Give them the things they need, or want, and the possession of these (material) things may make the needy 'happier' (and perhaps more self-respecting) up to a point: the same might be true of the luxury seekers. But it is up to them to 'make good'. Utilitarianism does not, in its formula 'each to count as one and no one to count for more than one' consider persons as persons, but as units in a computation.

Another connected point is that, in making actual results a determinant of moral rightness, this 'rightness' may depend on *luck*. Bernard Williams, in his book, *Moral Luck*,[1] has a long and interesting discussion on this issue. I can only refer to his examples here, and not to his subtle analysis. Gauguin abandoned his wife and family and went off to the Pacific to paint. His painting was a superb success, and Gauguin's judgement of his artistic capacities was right. But if the thing had turned out otherwise, would the 'morality' of his original decision be affected? Anna Karenina's judgement of the possible effects of her life with Vronsky on herself and on her son turned out to be wrong. If she had been right would the 'morality' of her action have been different? A scrupulously careful lorry driver, through no fault whatever of his, runs over a child. His remorse is agonizing. But do the actual results in any way affect our judgement of the man—or indeed should they affect even his *rational* judgement of himself? On the causal account of Utilitarianism strictly speaking they should. I (I imagine along with many other people) would disagree. 'Morality' belongs *within* the field of responsible judgement, motive and action. The factor of uncontrollable chance is not part of it. Certainly there is 'luck'. But not, I think, *'moral* luck'. (I must repeat here that these cursory remarks are not an attempt to deal with the problem of 'moral luck' as Professor Williams sees it in all its complexity.)

2. The division between right and good

Another aspect of the tendency to separate morality from its internal relation to the whole person of the moral agent is the division between right and good. It is inherent in Utilitarianism. As Mill has it: 'the motive has nothing to do with the morality of the act, though much to do with the worth of the agent'.[2] Since then, the emphasis on moral acts, duties, the right, out of intrinsic relationship with the person who acts, an emphasis which has dominated ethical discussion since the earlier years of the century, has distorted our conception of moral values. This deontological, rather than axiological, emphasis has been at the expense of consideration of good, goodness, the qualities of character. (Iris Murdoch's three essays, under the title of *The Sovereignty of Good*,[3] were, happily, a return to good as the centre of ethics and morality.)

Prichard and Ross, earlier in the century, sharply divided right from good. Ross brought out the distinction very clearly in his differentiation between 'right acts' and 'moral actions' which are expressive of good motives. In *The Right and the Good* he wrote:

> Clearance would be gained if we used the word 'act' of the thing done, the initiating of change, and the 'action' of the doing of it, the initiating of change, from a certain motive. We should then talk of a right act but not of a right action, of a morally good action but not of a morally good act. And it may be added that the doing of a wrong act may be a morally good action: for 'right' and 'wrong' refer entirely to the thing done, 'morally good' and 'morally bad' entirely to the motive from which it is done.[4]

On Ross's assumptions we can see the logic of his case but question the assumption. In a book, *Creative Morality*,[5] I wrote: 'Here, no less than in Prichard's theory, we have the *reductio ad absurdum* of a false abstraction. We are given the dissected pieces of a corpse when we should be trying to understand the behaviour of a living body.'* To this it should be added that both Prichard and Ross make a focal appeal to formal *reason* in their accounts of intuition (as Sidgwick[6] before them had done). As the apprehension that this is a three-sided figure immediately implies that it has three angles, so the apprehension that this is a promise implies that it ought to be kept. Or (for Ross) as in mathematics a predicate, though not included in the definition of the subject, necessarily belongs to anything which satisfies that definition, so with, for example, a promise. (The kind of criticism of this which has been applied to it is that it does not help us to understand *moral* obligation. If I make a promise and break it, my action contradicts the definition of a promise. It is logically wrong; but it still has to be shown that it is morally wrong to break the promise. If A treats B in a manner in which it would be wrong for B to treat A unless there are relevant differences between the natures or circumstances of the two, the 'wrong', though including the

---

* The style of this now sounds to me rude. This is the last thing I intended. Sir David was the soul of courtesy in his personal replies to me, and in his later *Foundations of Ethics* (Oxford: Oxford University Press, 1938).

inconsistency, is not shown to be morally wrong by the mere fact of the inconsistency.)

More recent writings, such as those of Rawls[7] and Kohlberg,[8] which focus their attention on right rather than good, and make *justice* the dominating concept of all morality, suffer from the same defect of an abstract intellectualism. Form is cut off from content; consistency, universalizability, comprehensiveness are centralized rather than concern for human welfare—or, if that is thought to be going too far, it is at least true that form is put *before* content, and that the justification of content is derived deductively from general principles.

3. Hare: reason versus feeling: the rational 'archangel'

Professor R.M. Hare could not be accused of not caring enough—and not caring deeply—about concrete human moral issues. In the Preface to *Moral Thinking*,[9] he begins:

> I offer this book to the public now rather than later, not because I think it needs no improvement, but because of a sense of urgency—a feeling that if these ideas were understood, philosophers might do more to help resolve important practical issues. These are issues over which people are prepared to fight and kill one another; and it may be that unless some way is found of talking about them rationally and with hope of agreement, violence will finally engulf the world.

And Hare has always laid great stress on the moral importance of bringing up a family. On the other hand he confesses to being 'passionate about reason' (and who am I to disagree on that?). The question is—and there has been much debate about his many writings—whether he manages to unite these two concerns coherently. Here, in this chapter of a book, I am making no attempt to examine critically Hare's philosophy, or the philosophies of the other writers I have mentioned: all of them have developed their views in great detail, and have replied to criticisms of them. Here I am concerned chiefly to try to prepare the way for the asking of one central question: 'What is the place of reason in a holistic conception of personal morality?'

I conceive of reason not as a single 'faculty', but as a central influence which can permeate and leaven the whole person, infusing his/her thoughts, feelings and actions with certain indefinable qualities.

The qualities are, in the end, being actual values, indefinable: and this is all metaphorical language. But in the end, in these things I think we may have to accept metaphor, even poetry.

A common metaphor of reason is to say that it is *paramount*. Paramount is what many philosophers past and present have conceived it to be. The metaphor has its point, but as usually conceived, it can be imaginatively too limited. It contains too strongly the image of 'above', superior, supreme over everything else and here supreme over feeling, desire, will, these being subservient to it. And it is a misleading metaphor, suggesting another, that reason and reasoning come *first*, feeling and will following them, *after*, obediently. If we must have metaphor, I think that 'leaven' is a better one, or any powerful influence working within, and through, and permeating, an organism. It is true that in some moral situations we retire to think and reason about what is good, or we ought to do in the circumstances. But here, though there is reflective thinking, some weighing and measuring and generalizing, it is thinking, with imagination, about particular things we feel and care about; and our thinking *is* a kind of feeling and caring, or is at least inseparable from these, though perhaps abstractly and analytically distinguishable from them. And what we call a 'reasonable' person is, surely, a person who thinks, chooses and acts in this way?

To return for a moment to Hare. With my one limited, though important, question in mind, I shall not attempt any criticism of Hare as a whole (he has replied in great detail to what he holds to be misconceptions of his views), or repeat familiar objections to his idea of morality as 'prescriptive', or as 'universalistic', or as utilitarian, the latter two symptomatic of his intellectualism. I note only one significant passage, in the chapter in *Moral Thinking*, 'The archangel and the prole'. The 'archangel' is

> a being with superhuman powers of thought, superhuman knowledge and no human weaknesses ... He will need to use only critical thinking. When presented with a novel situation he will be able at once to scan all its properties, including the consequences of alternative actions, and frame a universal principle (perhaps a highly specific one) which he can accept for action in that situation, no matter what role he himself were to occupy in it. Lacking, among other human weaknesses, that of partiality to self, he will act on that principle, if it bids him act ... Such an archangel would not need intuitive thinking; everything would be done by reason in a moment of time. Nor, therefore, would he need the sound general principles, the good dispositions, the intuitions which guide the rest of us.[10]

The 'prole', on the other hand (the term is borrowed from Orwell's *1984*) is a person who has these human weaknesses to a supreme degree. Not only does he, like most of us, have to rely on intuitions and sound prima facie principles and good dispositions for most of the time; he is totally incapable of critical thinking (let alone safe or sound critical thinking) even when there is leisure for it. Such a person, if he is to have the prima facie principles he needs, will have to get them from other people by education or imitation.[11]

Hare adds a caution:

it is far from my intention to divide up the human race into archangels and proles; we all share the characteristics of both to limited and varying degrees and at different times.

Our question then is, 'When ought we to think like archangels and when like proles?' Once we have posed the question in this way, the answer is obvious: it depends on how much each one of us, on some particular occasion or in general, resembles one or other of these two characters. There is no philosophical answer to this question; it depends on what powers of thought and character each one of us, for the time being, thinks he possesses. We have to know ourselves in order to tell how much we can trust ourselves to play the archangel without ending up in the wrong Miltonic camp as *fallen* archangels.[12]

The philosophical question is: how are the two kinds of thinking related to one another? Hare refers to Aristotle.

Aristotle, in a famous metaphor, says that the relation of the intellect to the character . . . has to be a paternal one: in so far as a man's motives and dispositions are rational, it is because they 'listen to reason as to a father'. Because intuitive moral thinking cannot be self-supporting, whereas critical thinking can be and is, the latter is epistemologically prior. *If* we were archangels, we could by critical thinking alone decide what we ought to do on each occasion; on the other hand, if we were proles, we could not do this, at least beyond the possibility of question, by intuitive thinking.[13]

This is a most interesting metaphor, and it illuminates Hare's position, showing it very clearly. And as such, I think it shows it to be completely *wrong*. Allowing for all the limitations of metaphor, and agreeing that we are neither archangels nor proles, I believe that Hare's idea that his moral thinking, and ours, should, as far as possible, aspire to the form of archangelic thinking, would result in a travesty of moral thinking and judgement. All archangels, he says,

at the end of their critical thinking, will all say the same thing, on all questions on which moral argument is possible; and so shall we, to the extent that we manage to think like archangels. Intuitive thinking has the function of yielding a working approximation to this for those of us who cannot think like archangels on a particular occasion.[14]

But the archangel is not a proper model for even an aspect of human moral judgement and decision. He has a fictionally high prestige as a purely rational being, but, as having no human weaknesses, nor any general moral principles, nor any good dispositions, and no *love*, he is certainly not a Christian archangel! He is, I would say, utterly *incompetent* to guide ordinary moral human understanding, judgement, decision. He is prescient of all the future as we are not. He has, it seems, no feelings; he does not care about moral ideals or principles or other human beings (and there are no 'others', for he is not one of them); he has no 'intuitions'—in Hare's very limited sense of intuitions derived from moral social upbringing. He has no particular ordinary experiences of value at all. He is an omniscient Calculator. His critical thinking is not *moral* thinking, for he is not a *person*, with his archangelic halo (I think it must be a square halo!). What sort of a model is this, even as a part of what human moral beings might aspire to be? (As for the thought-vacuous prole, he is a morally-conditioned automaton.)

Ordinary human beings, reasonably responsible moral agents, are, on the contrary, fallible persons among persons, born and living in contingency, with feelings and passions for good or evil, some thoughts about them, with necessarily limited understanding of the human situation past, present and future. The moral agent has to take chances, even in his/her most rationally supported moral judgements, with a realistic (and sometimes wry) acceptance that even in those most rationally supported moral judgements, he/she may be wrong not only in his/her calculations but even in his/her moral principles; for these need re-scrutiny. Incidentally, even Hare's reference to Aristotle's advice to 'listen to reason as to a father' can be misleading. For (without attempting a gloss on Aristotle's meaning) one's 'father' is not a wholly rational being. And if he is not, perhaps his *feelings* as a human father should come in too. If the 'relation of the intellect to the character has to be a paternal one' let the paternal influence be not *just* 'rational' in the limited sense, but fully human. In sum: 'critical thinking' is not, as Hare says, 'epistemologically prior' to intuitive moral thinking—it is subsequent. Hare is wrong in saying that critical (moral) thinking is 'self-supporting'. As Hegel says somewhere of Minerva (the patron symbol of reason and philosophy), 'The owl of Minerva takes her flight when the shades of night are falling.' Reason surveys Experience.

4. Respect for persons

Since Kant the principle of 'respect for persons' has been widely accepted by moralists as a central principle of ethics. For Kant the 'person' was a morally rational being, autonomous, able to give law universal to himself, to be respected as such. Since then the basis of 'respect' has been broadened by an attention to content as well as form, to the values or ideas of what is good and bad which a person holds and by which he/she lives. The 'person' we are adjured to respect is more concretely conceived and imagined. The term 'respect for a person' as commonly used has changed its meaning from being a purely rational respect by one rational being for another, to 'respect' for a person who embodies values of which we approve. Because these values and the person are so bound up together, we can only say (in this more concrete usage) that we respect a person whose values we approve of. The corollary of this is that we cannot say we 'respect' a person whose values we disapprove of so far as they are embodied in that person, values for which we may have contempt or which we loathe or despise. In this sense and use, I cannot honestly say that I 'respect' persons who habitually exploit human beings in their power, who deliberately set out to destroy young people's lives by selling them noxious drugs for profit, who torture for pleasure. Can we say that we 'respect as persons' the Nazi SS men? I think that in the sense in which we have been just using the word, we cannot.

But 'hard cases make bad law'. What has just been said does not, I think, in the least weaken the central importance of the principle of 'respect for persons'. It limits the scope of its practical application. We affirm the right of every person to a fair trial, for instance, however foul their alleged misdeeds. But because of them, the range of our outgoing sympathetic feeling is in the nature of things much restricted, and our 'respect' becomes formalized into a principle of the right to justice. Beyond that, however, there is still the principle of treating convicted evildoers as persons and not as things necessarily predetermined to continue in their own ways. As we said above (p. 70 *et sq.*) it is part of the definition of persons that they can ask questions, sometimes very ultimate ones, about their own lives. They are free as persons—even if convicted evildoers—to reflect. They *may*, on reflection on their past, see themselves in a new light. It is possible, and it sometimes happens, that a person is 'changed' after such reflection and becomes a very different kind of person. The treatment of a justly convicted person ought always to have this in mind.

The 'hard cases', then, do limit the scope of action as an expression of respect, but do not affect the principle itself. For the rest, the scope is wide open. Concern for human beings as personal (including of course oneself) is still a dominating principle of responsible moral life.

The principle of respect for persons, though given its content from experience, is of course still very formal and general; it does not in itself give any details for the conduct of everyday life. To think of the principle is to think primarily of a concept, or of a general good disposition. Even if one does not reduce it, as Kant does, to the concept of 'persons' as 'rational beings', it is still general. The distinction from Kant's view is nevertheless important. 'Respect', albeit a concept, is, on a more liberal view, a concept which though still general, is suffused with something more, a *feeling* for human persons as persons whom we know, concretely, as having—potentially at least—the range of qualities positive and negative, weaknesses and strengths, loveableness and hatefulness, of actual and real people. Many of the observations in Chapter VI apply here. We have variegated *images* of 'persons' derived from ordinary experiences, as well as just pure concepts of them. I shall return to this later, to the moral dispositions we can have and think we ought to have, towards real flesh-and-blood embodied persons.

5. The objectivity of moral good

Meanwhile there is the question of the objectivity of this moral good. I referred to it in the last chapter and shall only say what is necessary here, for it has been much written over.

I shall waive for the time being the question of the objectivity of the rightness of particular decisions which may be legitimately questioned—though without, I think, involving moral scepticism—and concentrate now only on the objectivity of moral good, the most fundamental question. This distinction between right and good is of the utmost importance, because the focus of the many contemporary discussions, and sceptical discussions, about objectivity, has been largely upon the objectivity of *right* decisions. But the root question is, can we have objective knowledge about moral good and bad (or evil)?

The question is admirably dealt with in Renford Bambrough's penetrating study, *Moral Scepticism and Moral Knowledge*,[15] to which I am indebted and in substantial agreement. He cites and discusses, *inter alia*, Hare, Nowell-Smith and Braithwaite (between 1952 and 1955). Later there have been sceptics like John Mackie in *Inventing Right and*

Wrong.[16] And of course there were the existentialist-subjectivist positions of Sartre and Gide, where moral choice is represented as arbitrary and totally 'free'. But 'choosing' ultimate principles (or what are to count as principles) will not do, as if—as Bambrough puts it—'it is possible for you to choose one set and me to choose another without its being the case that either is wrong in his choice'.[17]

Moral knowledge is centered, as I have already urged, on particular direct holistic experiences of human persons in factual situations. In such and such circumstances, can we say that *this* is, humanly speaking, inherently or intrinsically good, or bad (or evil)? We can. Here is a slave, a human person, bought for a pittance, a person bought as a thing, and, though a person sensitive to pain and indignity of all kinds, driven by fear of the whip or worse. Is this good, or is it evil? Answer, 'Evil'. Here is a small community living together in peace and harmony, with mutual consideration, trust, integrity, co-operation, love ... Is this good? Or bad? Answer, 'Good'. These questions and answers, perhaps insultingly naïve to intelligent readers, could be multiplied indefinitely. They can be extended of course to broad patterns of interpersonal living.

But though naïve, crude, platitudinous, such questions are crucial if their implications are taken seriously. A condition of my insistence that it is on particular experiences that valid judgements must be based was that the experience must not only be direct, but holistic. This means that it is an experience and judgement in which reason as well as knowledge of fact, and feeling (sometimes emotion), are all involved and function as a whole together. The feeling or emotion involved is not a private idiosyncratically coloured feeling or emotion, or a particular private wish or interest or prejudice which exists beforehand and colours the judgement, but a feeling or emotion sensitively objective and imaginative, one arising from the total objective judgement emanating from the objective contemplation of the situation itself. Of course selfishness or other bias can cloud judgements, or more often prevent a person from even trying to look objectively at a particular situation in which moral good or evil are involved. And if one invokes 'consensus' on some questions of good and evil which seem plain in what we may call a morally civilized society, it is consensus on matters which seem plain to all competent and unbiased observers in that society. The appeal to consensus is not an appeal merely to the counting of heads; the consensus arises out of a common experience of interpersonal good and, so far, is universal. As universal, the claim would be that such judgements apply to *all* persons and persons in relation, and are reasonable judgements.

And if anyone asks, perversely (as some people do), 'Why should I be objective and reasonable in my judgements when I don't want to be? Why should I think and be what I don't want to?', they are asking—if they are really seriously asking the question—for a reason, and so refuting their own question. Or if they are not serious they are opting out of rational moral discourse.

To claim that we have objective knowledge, as against the sceptics who affirm that we create our own moral values by deciding what counts as value, does not mean that we can claim to know good fully, adequately. There *are* many virtues which we can confidently categorize, as the outcome of common tested experiences of value widely shared—justice, truth, integrity, benevolence. . . These are common virtues and have as categories familiar general names. But as they only become actualized in particular examples, in the characters and actions of particular and individual persons, they acquire as so realized, something of an individual quality in each case, in some degree affected by the *Gestalt* of the particular person. Although this may go unnoticed—and does not ordinarily need to be noticed—the phenomenon can be seen to be important if we remember the essentially self-conscious nature of a 'person', how he/she is free and develops, not from some fully predetermined essence which unfolds inevitably, but from his/her reflections upon himself/herself, and values, and personal decisions.

Conceptually speaking, each virtue which is actualized can be said to be an instance of that category of virtue: but actual virtue is always much more than an instance of any category. It is the quality of a person expressed in his/her action, at his/her stage of personal moral development. It is a quality difficult, or more truly, impossible, to name exactly, and it requires maturity and sensitivity to appreciate. Furthermore, one cannot foresee, because it is free and personal, how such moral quality may develop, or, generally, how the depth and breadth of good may be measured.

6. Principles of good and rules of right

So far, good and its objectivity. It has been affirmed that respect for persons is a central principle and that this is a key to questions of moral action. But what about right and duty, discussed earlier in the chapter? In this section I shall raise one part of the question only and shall return to it much more fully later. The particular part of the question which I want to state now is that which arises from the opposition between those

who take what is commonly called an 'axiological' view of morality, and
the others who hold the 'deontological' theory. Broadly they stand for
emphasis on good or moral value on the one hand, and right and duty on
the other. I shall adopt an axiological standpoint.

Looking at it from the inside of moral experience, the moral
experience of a person who believes, perhaps passionately, in the
principle of respect for persons—what does he/she do when it comes to
particularities? How does he/she express this conviction and attitude in
particular and individual cases? What is the relation of what he/she
believes to be essentially *good* personal qualities and dispositions of a
person to the particularities of *right* action? Is he/she, when it comes to
the test of a difficult decision and action, a 'rule-governed' person? In
his/her order of things, does the realization of *good*, or the best (most
good) that can be realized in particular cases, have priority—where there
is conflict—over the weighing against one another, of given *rules* of
right? It is important to ask this question. One has often heard it said very
glibly 'Of course morality is rule-governed behaviour'. Clearly the
statement contains a truth. But it is stated as if this were the
distinguishing character of morality itself, instead of one facet of it only.
The important question is: what is to be the dominating guide of moral
life, perhaps final in cases of difficult conflict? Is it to be choice, finally,
from the set of accepted (and perhaps acceptable) prima facie principled
rules of right? Or is it to be responsible personal decision arising out of
convictions of and sentiments for *good*, directed to the concrete
particularities of *this* situation, the rules (which are abstractions) being
peripheral for the time being? Or, putting it in another way: is the
pattern of moral life dominated by the sense of importance of 'deontic'
acts, or by the importance of axiological, or what may be called 'areteic'*
actions? Axiology and deontology are two very different interpretations
of moral life.

7. The holistic apprehension of good

We have been reflecting critically upon current tendencies to think (in
effect) in separative 'faculty' terms about morals and moral values—of
intellectual 'reason' as a kind of Master over all, of reason divided off
from feeling and moral sentiments, of 'will' and motivation as something
else again, of right separated off from good. This critical note will be

* I take 'axiological' to be the more general word, referring to *value*, 'areteic' to *moral*
value or good.

continued: but I want now to suggest positively how habits of *holistic* thinking about morals lead to what seems to me to be a more realistic picture of what morality is about. I shall continue to concentrate mainly on our knowledge and understanding of the morally *good*, rather than (at present) on the more particular problems of how we know and understand what we mean by *right* acts and actions. This is not—as will be by now understood—because I think that these two areas, though distinguishable, are separable, but rather because, as I believe and shall try to show, that good is the central and dominating conception in ethics, and that right is its implementation in so far as possible and relevant in particular circumstances.

In Nicolai Hartmann's terms,[18] any principle of value contains the concept of 'ought'. (Here we are concerned with moral value and the moral 'ought'.) The 'ought-to-be' is distinguished from the 'ought-to-do'. The ought-to-be is basic, and does not logically imply the ought-to-do, which belongs to the realm of practice and the will. The ought-to-be is an ideal. We can affirm and believe that there ought to be (Kant's) 'perpetual peace', or good will between all men, and believe it to be unconditionally good, and yet by our individual actions be unable to realize it. The ought-to-be ought to be, irrespective of its actuality or even of its possibility. On the other hand our *apprehension* of the ideal ought-to-be contains a conative element. If we are deeply convinced that it is a state of affairs that ought to be, there is a *motive to do* anything we can to promote it, even if such doing is effectively minimal or perhaps nil. The complex concept of ought-to-be is in itself the exhibition of a tension between the concepts of what *is* and what *ought* to be. The tension is inherent in the very complexity of the concept itself of ought-to-be, even when, sometimes, ought-to-be is actually realized. That the goodwill between persons is sometimes realized, actually occurs, and *is*, does not contradict its ought-to-be. The actual tension within the ought-to-be is here, perhaps very temporarily, resolved practically in this situation; but the conceptual tension remains. That a person ought to be honest, straightforward, trustworthy, is something which does not cease to be because somebody actually is so. The person ought to be even as he/she then is. This is not a tautology.

The point that the ought-to-be contains a *nisus* towards being, and our *apprehension* of the ought-to-be a *conative* element, a desire, longing, a want that it should be so, is of essential importance when we move from the realm of the ought-to-be to the ought-to-do. It is shown in the instance of trying to do what we can, even if the effect is minimal or nil.

In other cases, when some effective action *is* within our practical scope and power, the conative or motivational element in our apprehension of good as ought-to-be, becomes essential. The content of our judgement of what we ought to do here and now is of course relative to, partly determined by, the nature of the particular concrete situation in which action is called for—its possibilities, likely effects, and so on. But it is the general directing sentiment for the ought-to-be, with its built-in motive for potential action, which is a fundamental overall dynamic influence on the pattern and quality of practical moral life.

Terms like ought-to-be and ought-to-do are of course highly abstract and general. Necessary and important abstractions they are: but if we accept them, our full acceptance is not merely the detached intellectual acceptance of them as stateable concepts, but is inseparable from the feeling for them, from conation, from the feeling and will that the ought-to-be should *be*, and that the ought-to-do should be *done*. Furthermore, this totalistic acceptance is the fruit of equally totalistic concrete experience, sometimes actual, sometimes imagined. Whether the concrete experience of good as ought-to-be is of this as actually realized in some living example or examples of it, or is *imagined* as being realized, what is essential is the involvement of the whole person, and not merely the 'intellect'. Actual or imagined, the cognitive apprehension has to be fully *imaginative*.

Many contemporary writers on morals, we noted, seem to sit very loosely to the necessity of a holistic approach to the knowledge and understanding of moral values. Hare, though he can be described as intellectualist-formalistic in tendency, making universalizability and the utilitarian calculus central for mature morals, does lay great stress on the influence of parents and teachers in the upbringing of children, as forming what he calls (but in his limited sense of the word) 'intuitions' or 'prima facie principles' which are associated, owing to our upbringing, with very firm and deep dispositions and feelings. But they do not, in the context of his thinking, give moral *knowledge*: they reinforce, give motive power to 'prescriptions'. John Wilson pays some formal tribute to 'what psychologists (rather regrettably) call the "affective" area', and he includes in his scheme for moral education, 'emotional awareness'.[19] He labels it EMP. But for Wilson the intellectual emphasis is primary: '"the intellectual" aspect is to mark out what morality is uniquely about ...' The central component is intellect (PHIL), and emotional awareness secondary. In what Hare calls 'descriptivist' (as opposed to 'prescriptivist') ethics, the same mistake occurs—of not clearly distinguishing the moral from the logical—as we saw in the earlier Ross (page 86). Kohlberg[20] has spoken (as a formalist) rather contemptuously of the 'bag of moral virtues'. The opening sentence of a paper given at a conference in 1978 by Charles Bailey[21] is: 'This paper argues that morality is largely to do with reason and little to do with feelings and the affective.' The affirmation in the statement is acceptable up to a point: the denial far too sweeping.

If for the moment we leave generalizations and consider how, as quite ordinary moral human beings, we look at, appreciate, judge, of the goodness-claims of various common values such as charitableness, justice, compassion, as they occur in actual or imagined moral life, it may suggest or show how clipped, dried up, 'academic' in (I think) the bad sense, are the approaches cited in the last paragraph. As examples I will take, not actual occurrences, but imagined ones. They are parables of the New Testament, with titles familiar to at least every literate person of the West. Beyond those titles, I fear that one cannot assume that the actual stories, written in language of telling simplicity in the Authorised Version of the New Testament, are familiar at least to 'every literate person of the West'! I shall therefore quote extensively from the biblical text.

The stories are of The Good Samaritan (Luke 10, 25–37) and of The Prodigal Son (Luke 15, 11–32).

In the Good Samaritan story it must be understood (as we are told in St John) that 'the Jews have no dealings with the Samaritans'. In the Samaritan story, a Jewish lawyer quotes the Jewish Law: 'Thou shalt love the Lord thy God with all thy heart, and with all thy soul, and with all thy strength, and with all thy mind; and thy neighbour as thyself.' (Note the 'faculty' comprehensiveness of this!) And, to 'test' Jesus, he asks, 'And who is my neighbour?'

The answer is in the parable. A certain man (a Jew) 'fell among thieves, which stripped him of his raiment, and wounded him, and departed, leaving him half dead.' Two Jews pass that way; each, when they saw him, 'passed by on the other side'. (Both Jews lived according to the 'Law', one a priest, the other a Levite.)

> But a certain Samaritan, as he journeyed, came where he was: and when he saw him, he had compassion on him, and went to him, and bound up his wounds, pouring in oil and wine, and set him on his own beast, and brought him to an inn, and took care of him. And on the morrow when he departed, he took out two pence, and gave them to the host, and said unto him, 'Take care of him; and whatsoever thou spendest more, when I come again, I will repay thee.'

Jesus asks: 'Which now of these three, thinkest thou, was neighbour unto him that fell among the thieves?' The lawyer replies: 'He that shewed mercy on him.' Then said Jesus unto him, 'Go, and do thou likewise.'

In the Prodigal Son story, a younger son asks his father for the portion of the inheritance due to him, goes off to a far country, wastes his substance in riotous living, starves in a famine, is driven to feed swine, can hardly fill his belly 'with the husks that the swine did eat'. In desperation he ruminates:

> How many hired servants of my father's have bread enough and to spare, and I perish with hunger! I will arise and go to my father, and will say unto him, 'Father, I have sinned against heaven, and before thee, and am no more worthy to be called thy son: make me as one of thy hired servants.' And he arose, and came to his father. But when he was yet a great way off, his father saw him, and had compassion, and ran, and fell on his neck, and kissed him. And the son said unto him, 'Father, I have sinned against heaven, and in thy sight, and am no more worthy to be called thy son.' But the father said to his servants, 'Bring forth the best robe, and put it on him; and put a ring on his hand, and shoes on his feet: and bring hither the fatted calf, and kill it; and let us eat and be merry: for this my son was dead, and is alive again; he was lost, and is found.'

But the elder son from the fields hearing the sounds of music and dancing, called one of the servants to explain.

> And he was angry, and would not go in: therefore came his father out, and intreated him. And he answering said to his father, 'Lo, these many years do I serve thee, neither transgressed I at any time thy commandment: and yet thou never gavest me a kid, that I might make merry with my friends: but as soon as this thy son was come, which hath devoured thy living with harlots, thou hast killed for him the fatted calf.' And he said unto him, 'Son, thou art ever with me, and all that I have is thine. It was meet that we should make merry, and be glad: for this thy brother was dead and is alive again; and was lost, and is found.'

These stories, vividly told, perhaps show how far a holistic approach is necessary to understand and to know the qualities of moral goodness. (The Prodigal Son parable also illustrates the puzzles involved in judging what is morally 'right'.)

In both stories the qualities of love and compassion are very clearly shown. In the Good Samaritan parable they are contrasted with the rigid ingrown legalism of the priest and the Levite: Our question is, 'How do we "know" and understand (in so far as we can be said in some degree to know and understand) the goodness of the qualities of love and compassion?'

Questions of universalizability or the hedonic calculus do not directly or relatively arise here. Nor is a merely 'intellectual' approach (Wilson's PHIL) anything like adequate, even if slightly garnished from the 'affective area' with some 'emotional awareness'. Nor does the 'logic' that entails that a promise—or a contract written or assumed—having been made, 'must' be kept, really touch the elder son's *moral* grievance against his father. The *content*, the actual quality of the good of compassion and love, is what here supremely matters, and it must be apprehended intuitively, directly. To consign it, with a sort of implicit contempt, as an item to be popped into a 'bag of [stereotyped] virtues' is to abdicate from the responsibility of trying to understand love and compassion.

Certainly our upbringing and the climate of the moral culture in which we live, do, very importantly, count in our appreciation and assessment of what is morally good. If we are brought up by our parents and teachers to consider other people, to respect truthfulness, sincerity, faithfulness, justice ... and in a society which, on the whole approves of these excellences, we will, as responsible thinking adults, tend—if the strains are not too great!—to be biased towards them. If our culture is Fascist-dominated, or impregnated by fanatical religion, religiously intolerant, where violence and brutality are accepted as normal or even desirable, our responses and judgements will tend to be the polar opposite. Toleration will be thought weak, compassion merely sentimental. Physical coercion will be accepted, efforts to rational persuasion inept.

But though these latter attitudes may well be the effect of sheer conditioning, the former, if they are to be really morally viable, are not. If, in the setting of the more humane environment, we are being merely conditioned to 'think', 'feel', be emotionally disposed by drill and habit to certain beliefs and attitudes which are socially approved by one's society, the resulting 'morality', though it may be correctly conventional and rule-abiding, will have no real moral grip. Only if, from the earliest days, and suitably adjusted as we grow up, our moral education is grounded in holistic, sensitively *imaginative* experience of concrete moral values, will it develop into genuine moral understanding and knowledge. This will certainly be *rational*, including intellectual understanding of the structure of moral situations, of the effects and likely results of practical decisions. It will be aware of the ways in which moral decisions and moral values arise out of, are affected by, and affect, matters of *fact*. Rational judgement is intelligent, involves all-round intellectual appraisal of fact-value situations. But as 'rational' it is far more than intellectual. As with all value-understanding, feeling, cognitive and affective, is built in to its very apprehension, and the personal mind must act as one. The cognitive-conative-affective (and sometimes emotion) combine in a *total* moral percipience. This may be called a 'holistic rationality'.

We have been concentrating on the knowledge and understanding of moral *good*, and I am not here and now directly concerned with *rightness* of moral acts and actions. But of course this is involved all the time in practical moral life. It shows itself in the parable of the Prodigal Son, though we have to remember that this is a parable, a picturesque piece of moral propaganda. The parables of Jesus are prophetic paradoxes, bringing out moral points of great importance: taken as literal prescriptions they would often be impossible to implement, or morally wrong. In the Prodigal story, the elder son certainly has a point. He was, very understandably, angry: it was not fair or just that his reprobate younger brother should be given all the honours, and the fatted calf, when he, the faithful and virtuous had not, all these years, been given even a kid! And perhaps his father had taken him too much for granted? ('Son, thou art ever with me, and all that I have is thine.') If this were a real-life situation rather than a parable, we might have to judge whether, in all the relevant circumstances, the father did the 'right' thing. The *principles* of the 'goods' of love and justice do not conflict, considered as general, abstracted from any particular context; each has its independent goodness. When it comes to action, they can conflict, and practical questions do arise. Is the love expressed in the words: 'This thy brother was dead and is alive again; and was lost, and is found', of greater importance in this situation than the claims of strict justice? This is the challenge of the parable.

8. 'Supererogation' and duty

Goodness (when it exists) is a quality of personal character and of characteristic actions directly or indirectly expressive of it. 'Morality' centred in good and goodness, I have called axiological (or areteic) as distinguished from morality centred on duty, rules of right—'deontological' morality. I have used inverted commas for areteic 'morality', because although it is certainly morality, its range is wider than what is ordinarily thought of as 'moral', doing one's duty, fulfilling obligations generally formulated and epitomized in prima facie rules, backed perhaps by formal principles of universalizability or by utilitarian principles of maximum satisfaction or happiness. Broadly, deontic morality stresses rule-governed *acts*. Broadly, areteic morality does not; its *actions* are more indicative of a whole form or style of life.

This contrast I think is very important, so long as it is not exaggerated. Deontic morality has its conceptions of 'good', areteic morality its conceptions of 'rules', 'duties' and 'right'. But in the two contexts the implications of the words 'good', 'rules', 'duties', 'right' are rather different. This is brought out in discussions of 'works of supererogation'. Professor Urmson raised this (very ancient) question again in a paper on 'Saints and heroes'.[22] Hare discusses it in *Moral Thinking*,[23] and it has been treated again in a short paper by Elizabeth Pybus.[24]

The issue is opened up by Jesus. In a passage where he suggests that people doing their ordinary duties need not be 'thanked' (or praised) for doing them, he goes on to say: 'So likewise ye, when ye shall have done all those things which are commanded you, say, "We are unprofitable servants: we have done that which was our duty to do." ' (Luke 17.10.) 'Duty' here seems to refer to the ordinary everyday duties which we accept and do without thinking much about them. (It *could* also refer to more exacting 'duties'.) Acts of supererogation are defined as acts which go beyond ordinary duties and are supposed to be praiseworthy though they are not obligatory. That there are, on the common assumptions about 'duties', acts which can be so described, is certainly true. Elizabeth Pybus sums up Urmson's usage of the terms 'saint' and 'hero'.

> A person is called a saint if he performs actions far beyond the limits of duty, either by control of contrary inclinations and interest, or effortlessly, and a hero if he performs actions beyond the bounds of duty either by controlling natural fear, or effortlessly. A man would be a saint in this sense if he volunteered to give medical aid in a plague-ridden city. He would be a hero in this sense if he sacrificed his life to save others by throwing himself on a live grenade.[25]

There are, then, such noble people and noble acts; and the acts are supererogatory in the sense defined: they 'pay out beyond what is expected'. (Concise O E D.) They are certainly beyond our 'duties' in one sense. But are they so on *any* interpretation of 'duty'?

It is interesting to look at the different ways of dealing with this question by the three authors mentioned. Urmson thinks that acts of supererogation are most certainly moral, but as they go beyond duties in the ordinary sense, they belong to a higher order or realm of morality, the realm of supererogation. They are not 'duties'. Hare distinguishes between common prima facie duties (which he calls 'principles'), morally obligatory to *all* in society, and 'principles' which are special, 'which are desirable in those who occupy certain roles, or vocations in the professional sense, like that of the doctor or lawyer or jobbing builder. And they will also include principles proper to my vocation in a much more personal sense, akin to that which it has in theology.'[26] These are 'principles', but for us as particular individuals, and not general for everybody. And he adds a comment, in his characteristic language.

> I have argued that, if we were bringing up a child purely in his own interest, we should try to inculcate into him some *prima facie* moral principles, with the attendant moral feelings. Will these include only the run-of-the-mill principles, or should more exacting principles be also absorbed, if it is within his capacity to live by them? I would answer 'Yes'; for it does look as if people who set themselves higher moral standards which are within their capacity, or not too far outside it, are in general happier than those who do not set their sights so high. But this is an empirical judgement for which I am not able to offer hard evidence; I can only ask the reader whether, from his own experience of life, he does not agree with it.[27]

In view of a comment I shall make below, I ask my reader to note certain words or phrases in this quotation. They are: 'his own interest', 'the attendant moral feelings', 'more exacting principles', 'are in general happier'.

Elizabeth Pybus argues that 'duty' covers the whole range of life and moral obligation, and includes therefore what is called the supererogatory, for all and each of us, within our capacities and powers. She urges that 'we should resist the view that there is a realm of moral aspiration beyond duty (or obligation)'[28] and says that Urmson is, in distinguishing between a morality of duty and a morality of aspiration, 'unnecessarily lowering the concept of duty'.[29] With important reservations about the use of the term 'duty' which I shall explain, I have sympathy with this view.

All three writers seem to want a more liberal idea of morality than the word 'duty' expresses, *if* the word is exclusively identified with the commonly accepted everyday duties. So do I. Urmson deals with the problem by affirming supererogation as separate from, and above, duties in the ordinary sense. But Hare seems to want to confine the demand of the 'more exacting' duties to those who have 'the capacity' (and set by 'vocation' of one sort or another) to live by them—and these persons are in a hypothetical minority. In this respect he would be opposed by Pybus, who thinks that 'duty' should cover the whole range of moral obligation, therefore rejecting supererogation.

Hare's liberality is, I think, a bit loose. What does he mean by bringing up a child 'purely in his own interest'? Are 'moral feelings' just 'attendant'? And is the empirical point that if people have higher aspirations they are 'in general happier' really relevant to an outgoing moral attitude? Is not Hare's account of morality with all his formal tests, a diluted one?

The question of supererogation arises in the context of a duty-oriented conception of ethics. For those who hold the supererogatory position (for example, Urmson) there are supererogatory actions which go beyond duty in the ordinary sense. On a consistent duty ethics (Pybus), duty covers the whole field of possible moral actions. I think it is useful, in all cases perhaps, but particularly on a view like that of Pybus, to distinguish between 'duties' in the ordinary run-of-the-mill sense (paying debts, keeping promises, telling the truth, etc.) and a general and overarching sense of 'Duty', pervading the whole range of moral life—and deserving a capital 'D'. Whichever view one holds, it is accepted as a fact that there are examples of moral actions which do go beyond the run-of-the-mill duties. To do this they need not be 'saintly' or 'heroic'; and I think the pitch is somewhat queered by thinking only of extreme examples. An ordinary neighbour, for instance, can, in kindness, go far beyond 'paying out what is expected' (OUD), and yet be far from being a 'saint'.

All this (to repeat) arises on a duty-centred perspective of ethics—on the Judaic-law ethic in the time of Jesus, and on the prevailing view of moral philosophy of at least the last fifty years. But how does it all look from an axiological, from what I have called an 'areteic', or what might now be called with equal cogency an 'agapistic' perspective? How, on this different view, would we see the ordinary 'duties', or the overarching 'Duty'?

9. Agape, Duty and duties

On an axiological view, duties and Duty are *derivative* notions. They arise in the context of a moral good-centred perspective. In a purely ideal world—and not in the ordinary human world as we know it—there would be no need for duties, and perhaps not even for Duty, at all. If, in our era, the conception of agape is derived from a theological idea of the love (agape) of God, and if we were all 'sons of God' in a complete and full sense, then in this purely fictional and ideal world, there would be no need for Duty or duties because all moral actions would be inspired by pure agape. As St Augustine put it, 'dilige et quod vis fac'. Needless to say the world as we know it has no resemblance at all to this ideal fiction—and I have referred to the fiction only in order to bring out the need for 'Duty' and 'duties' in any ordinary human context. Whether in the world-we-know there is, in fact, more evil will than good will, or more good will than evil, is fortunately a question that we do not even have to try to decide. There is a plenitude of weak, bad, evil . . . will to be getting on with—and which makes the notions of duties and Duty indispensable in any moral thinking.

Duties, on an areteic-agapistic perspective of morals, are part of the everyday circumstances of life, and in the mature person are so interwoven with it that the perfomance of 'duties' is often, or usually, quite automatic, and a 'duty' is hardly even thought of as such. Of *course* one keeps one's promises to the best of one's abilities, tells the truth, shows common courtesies, etc. Only when there are breaches may the question of 'fulfilling a duty' arise. And Duty, the general inclusive sentiment for which is built-in to character, takes general charge and keeps general order. It is only when—as may constantly happen—the general outgoing drive of agapistic arete is weak, or where there is some contrary drive, of prejudice, dislike, competing interest; or sheer natural laziness or inertia . . . that the need to call upon sense of Duty arises. The gap between what is and what ought-to-be must then be bridged by will.

But there is a great difference between a mature developed sense of Duty conceived in the areteic context, as the servant of a developed sentiment of respect, goodwill, care for persons as persons, and Duty set up as the *central* concept of morals. The difference stands out most sharply where, as in the contrasting philosophies of J.S. Mill and W.D. Ross, the motive is separated from the act. There, dutiful acts stand out coldly from motives, even from motives of duty. But even in the more usual duty-morality where the motive of duty is included in the moral valuation of the action, the difference between purely duty-motivated actions and actions areteically-motivated, a difference in moral 'style', seems very clear.

In the case of everyday run-of-the-mill duties, the source of the duty-motive in duty-morality is acknowledgement of the authority of the customary rules of morality, particular rules (promise-keeping, truth-telling, etc.) embodying a common moral tradition, let us say, of a particular civilized society. Conformity to them is reasonably to be expected. The same goes, as I have already suggested, for areteic morality, at least up to a point. But I think that the justifying reasons for accepting these rules, would be found at a deeper level to be different.

This is too complex to argue for here. But what I have in mind is that, in a very common way of thinking, the justification for the ordinary rules of morality lies in social amenity and convenience. The justification is, broadly speaking, a 'higher' convenience, a safeguard of social amenity so that society can run smoothly and with the least amount of friction. Duty-morality is founded on *mores*, though critically and reflectively. This may be contested as unfair: but in so far as it is true, it stands in contrast to areteic morality where the good of *persons* and persons-in-relation, intrinsically and as such, is central. On this view, to break promises without good reason, to lie, to use power with lack of consideration, is to treat persons (including oneself) as less than persons (cf. Chapter VI, page 70 *et sq.*). It is wrong to break promises, to lie, to exploit, because it degrades persons and relations between persons. Conformity to the ordinary duties is (for the most part unconsciously) motivated by a general sentiment for interpersonal good.

In strictest duty-morality, conformity to the common rules is simply acting out an *instance* of a general rule. In areteic morality conformity to common rules may look just like this. But, as I have suggested, on a deeper interpretation, rule-following is not simply the instantiation of a general socially prescribed moral rule, but, ultimately, an *expression* of personal concern. More generally, duty-morality's stress is upon *form*. Areteic morality is founded on a specific interpretation of *content*.

In most duty-rule-following there is no conflict. But sometimes there is, and it can on occasion be agonizing. And it seems to me that there is a difference in kind and quality between conflict in duty-centred, and in areteic morality.

10. Moral conflicts, axiological and deontic: two 'styles'

It is perhaps as well to point out that the phrase 'conflict of principles' commonly employed in this kind of discussion can be misleading. Principles of good (as I have used the term) in themselves cannot conflict. Dispositions of character as just, merciful, respecting truth, considerate, compassionate . . . remain, as qualities of character, always good. It is only when they are turned into *rules* of duty or right acts: 'Act justly, mercifully; speak the truth, act compassionately, *always*' that inevitable conflict—conflict of *duties*—arises. And it is, I think, a *mistake* and a confusion to turn principles of good, which, as dispositions are general, into rules of action, which must operate always in very particular circumstances. Rather one comes, with principled dispositions, to very particular situations of conflict, and has to make a fresh particular judgement, in the light of the circumstances. And it is here that the differences between the 'duty' and the 'areteic' approaches arise. Without going into the enormous variety of practical moral conflicts— which personal experience, literature, the daily press, can illustrate endlessly—one may venture the following. In both cases the conflict is 'personal' in the sense that it involves persons-having-to-decide-what-to-do. But if the decision is painful or difficult, the concentration, on the deontic view, will be upon which rule, as between conflicting rules of right or duty, to follow. On the areteic stance, on the other hand, decision is not basically dominated by given rules (however important they may be in their place), but by the influence of direct holistic influence and reflective conviction of the intrinsic moral goods from which the moral validity of the rules is derived. Since this conviction is fused into character and sentiments, penetrating into everything that is thought and felt and desired and done, the intensity of the conflict is far more deeply personal: there is a personal moral involvement of a kind which is different from the deontic rule-governed involvement.

The *range* of choice is wider on the areteic than on the duty view. 'Duties' are significantly selected clips from the panorama of human experience and its obligations. Duty, on both views, comprehends more than duties. But if, as was argued in the last chapter, agape is, so far as it is functioning well, characterized by feelingful as well as objective insight, it could well be expected (especially where personal issues were involved) to apprehend, in depth as well as in breadth, the complexity of situations of conflict holistically, as a more simply general-rule-governed approach could not do in the same way. Agape when in operation is more flexible and spontaneous, sensitive to conflicting claims, and at the same time 'disinterested' and rationally objective, in ways in which the more calculative weighing up of duties one against the other can hardly be. It is in a sense unbounded. This is why, perhaps (as I suggested) the intensity of conflict may be more deeply felt—and most of all when there seems to be no 'right' answer.

Professor Dorothy Emmet in her book *The Moral Prism*,[30] writes of morality as a three-stranded cord, the three strands intertwining. The strand which is relevant here is the third, which she calls the 'Generosity' strand. (Her 'Generosity' is very much akin to what I have referred to as agape.) It is 'generous action of a directly personal kind. This stands partly for the quest for an elusive ideal which cannot be contained in any set of rules.' It is not a calculating morality, however fair and reasonable such calculations may be. 'It stands for a highly personal kind of behaviour, which certainly cannot be prescribed in any set of rules, or can be expected of right.' It ranges from the morality of saints and heroes, to 'uncovenanted gracious acts of kindness where people are prepared, freely and ungrudgingly, not always to stand on their rights.'[31] She speaks, again, of 'a general slant or style of life in which one sets oneself to do whatever one does rather than as objectives to which one can take means'[32]—as in utilitarianism, for instance.

It is two 'styles' of moral life which I have been trying to describe: and it must be now clear which I prefer. I will only add that it is *styles* or *types* of moral life which I have been describing. I am not suggesting that real people in their moral dispositions and actions must exactly conform to one type or another. Perhaps some people do: some are much more of one type than the other: most of us are mixtures. The difference is between what is generally called an axiological and a deontological morality, one form of the axiological being agapistic. But it would be monstrous to suggest that any *person* calling themselves 'deontologist' would, in some situations of conflict, be therefore less humane, less sensitive to human good.

Axiological morality is *expressive* of good. Should it be called, as I called it in my previous book,[33] 'creative'? I am not sure. It is clear to me, as I tried to show, that *art* is genuinely creative. But it would be very difficult to argue similarly about morality, and difficult to find wholly convincing examples, as one can in art. There may be something which is called by some people an 'art' or a 'poetry' of living. But though this may occur here and there, I certainly do not want to say that all axiological morality is 'poetic'. Nor, though affirming that axiological morality is expressive, am I denying that *persons* who favour the deontological pattern are 'expressing' their own point of view, or that, as persons, they are precluded from having their possibly 'creative' moments. It is *types or styles* which are being contrasted, not the particular behaviour of particular persons. I certainly think that as a style or type of living axiological morality is more expressive in the sense described, than is deontological morality, and more hospitable, perhaps, to the idea of 'creative' moments. And there, in this open state, I now leave it.

Chapter VIII
Education and Ways of Understanding—Intellectual, Religious, Moral, Aesthetic

Behind any of the many particular questions which can arise within the very complex field of education—or, more broadly, the bringing up of children at home or at school—there are always some general assumptions about what this 'education' is *for*. What is it for during childhood and schooldays? And how does it relate to the long life after school?

These are absurdly simplified questions, and any attempt to develop answers to any of them spills over into a thousand particularities, philosophical, empirical, normative. The body of literature in philosophy, psychology, sociology of education, as well as educational history, mainly consists of the discussion of these things, in addition to popular views at every level which appear in the daily and weekly press. Parents and teachers are enmeshed in them at the level of ground experience. Here, however, I shall keep the picture deliberately broad and merely offer some reflections in the light of what has gone before in the book.

1. 'Aims of education'

There seem to be three main, but overlapping, emphases in talk of the aims of education. One emphasis is instrumentalist, held by a good many 'men in the street', increasingly by some politicians and some writers on education, that the main business of school education is to prepare children to be functionaries in whatever sort of adult society lies in wait for them. Another view focuses more on the importance of developing certain *particular* qualities in young people growing up—qualities physical, mental, affective and emotional, social, moral ... with a particular stress on one or another. A third would claim to be more comprehensive: the main aim of education should be the 'development of the whole person'. It is easy to be pretentious about this: for what is 'the *whole* person'? School education is only a part of education and a beginning. It is more modest, and realistic, to say education which *involves* the whole person.

The first, instrumentalist, view can be stated in moderate or in extreme forms. No sensible person denies that we are functionaries as well as persons, and that any idea of education which ignored the sort of pattern of adult life and culture into which children and adolescents will be initiated, would be irresponsible and absurd. Every statement of the aims of education must contain, to be valid, an instrumentalist factor, implicit or explicit. But this inclusion in itself does not make anyone who agrees to it an 'instrumentalist'. How far it can legitimately be so called will depend on how far the treatment of children as potential functionaries includes proper respect for them as persons. In other words it will turn on how far educating is fully accepted as a *moral* responsibility.

Sometimes, at least by implication, it is not. The assessment of the values of education in terms of 'cost-effectiveness', of defined predetermined 'objectives' of efficiency, is clearly instrumentalist in emphasis. The emphasis, quite common among parents, politicians and others, is legitimate up to a point. 'Accountability' in some sense is a fair claim. But these ambiguous words are extremely dangerous if they are used in contexts simply of politics, or economics, or business or commercial management, or even examination success, or of any image of human beings which, even covertly, conceives of them as merely units to be manipulated by some higher authority of whatever sort. And there is no doubt that ideas of this do in fact influence current discussions of the future of education, though they are generally well camouflaged—or offset—in this country, where there still, fortunately, remains a very active and articulate influence of humanitarianism. But the camouflage wears thin at points.

In America, the widespread influence of radically behaviouristic psychology has made it possible to proclaim boldly and openly, and without any camouflage at all, what can only be called an anti-human gospel of education. Needless to say, there are, among concerned American educationists, anguished protests against it. I quote from an article in the American journal *The Educational Forum* by Millard Clements, 'Performance based education: a social alchemy'.

'Critical words', Millard Clements says, 'in social alchemy are input, output, process, systems design, operational definition, behavioural terms, feed-back, and terminal objectives.' He quotes:

> A systems approach is essential to decision making in our highly complex world. The use of systems theory and analysis will enable us to see education and the activities of educators as a whole, to recognise how the various functions of educational organisations and operations depend on one another, and, finally, to understand how a change in any one part affects all components of the system . . . The systems approach begins by considering all potential programmatic plans in terms of broad goals and their more specific objectives, plus the interdependent activities needed to achieve the product desired. A system has been defined as a set of components organized in such a way as to constrain action towards the accomplishment of the purposes for which the system exists . . . An educational program is essentially an effort to process input to achieve output of a product with necessary feedback mechanisms . . .[1]

Clements goes on to say that another writer, Frederick J. McDonald, clarified the fundamental political conceptions in this way:

> Education is a process or an activity which is directed at desirable changes in the behaviour of human beings . . . An educational objective is a statement of a desired behavioural change, that is, it is a statement about the behaviour that shall be acquired by the child . . . The function of the learning experience is to evoke the desirable responses, to strengthen these responses, and to hasten the weakening of undesirable responses . . . The teacher in making decisions is, in a general sense, manipulating and controlling the child's behaviour.[2]

Clements comments on the pseudo-scientific character of this plunge into technocracy. That social alchemy *will* lead to the reform and regeneration of education is a matter of faith: there is no evidence whatever that it will. (If the 'alchemy' metaphor is followed, one might say that the 'systems' approach is more like an attempt to turn gold into base metal!) Clements makes several observations, interesting in the context of this book. One is on the externality of the relations between human beings which this view sets up as a principle. 'Systems managers and people are thought to belong to different orders of social reality: people are caught up in the web of life, but professionals dispassionately observe and compassionately manage the affairs of others.' (I query the 'compassionately'.) Another comment: 'What is new today is that this ancient predisposition of the strong to manage the weak is becoming implicit in our fundamental ways of *knowing*. It is becoming intelligent and even scientific to think of people as though they were things.' (Italic mine.) And, 'Knowledge is divorced from human struggle and made to appear to be simple linguistic expressions that are convenient for the design of behavioural investigations of education.' A 'psychologized knowledge exists apart from individual efforts. It can be recorded on file cards, in storage banks, and on computer print-outs.'

It is unnecessary for me to comment further on 'instrumentalist' theories of education. I have devoted some space to them to indicate, by implication and without additional argument, that they are not alternative philosophical theories of *education*, but morally irresponsible programmes of human conditioning, morally irresponsible because they are in effect anti-personal.

The second broad emphasis in thinking about education, I suggested, is on the importance of developing certain *particular* qualities in young people growing up. The emphasis may be religious, or on moral character, or 'social' (in several senses), or on the development of physical, or intellectual, or affective and emotional qualities. I stress 'emphasis', because of course these qualities overlap and get mixed up. But one can readily call to mind the religious foundations of many schools in this country: 'Christianity'; in the older 'public schools' the 'Christian gentleman'. This again was associated with the ability to mix and get on—with people in your own class anyhow—or, instrumentally, to be a leader of some sort in the adult world. The *physical* emphasis could be spartan. In the early years of the century, Loretto (east of east-windy Edinburgh) was almost unbearably cold, a place of always open windows and icy cold baths—done, of course, with 'moral' intent! In most public schools games are still a religion, sometimes with athletics and field and country sports. Gordonstoun and Outward Bound direct physical energies to training for human and social ends such as rescue work. Other schools, like Bryanston under Coade, stressing the imaginative, and the life of feeling, cultivate the arts, crafts, literature and music. Winchester and Manchester Grammar School are noted for their emphasis on mind and intellect. Let me say here that I have cited 'public' schools, because being more independent of general democratic public control and opinion, it is easier for them to develop independent lines, and, sometimes, to experiment in very radical ways, as at Neill's Summerhill, or Dartington.

2. 'The development of reason'

Since my own retirement in 1962 from the Chair of Philosophy of Education in the University of London, there has been great stress, as a main aim of education, on the development of reason. One has only to glance at the titles of books published in the 1970s, and some of the articles in them. There is the introductory work by Hirst and Peters in 1970, *The Logic of Education.*[3] There is the three-volume work, *Education and the Development of Reason,*[4] the middle volume of which, *Reason,* contains, among others, some very fine articles on reason, reasonableness, rationality, objectivity and truth, and practical reason. There is Hirst's book of collected papers, *Knowledge and the Curriculum,*[5] on meaning, knowledge, language, thought. There are others in the same vein. The general level of thinking in all these works is first-rate, and they have been enormously influential. The points of view expressed are of course individual and cannot be summed up in any formula. As Professor Peters, answering critics of the 'Malet Street School', observed: 'It is not a monolithic system.'

On the other hand, the emphasis has been one-sided. I suppose it would be agreed everywhere that the development of knowledge and understanding is a main aim of education, and that the development of reason is a central and essential factor in their development. But in the minds of philosophers brought up in the particular analytic tradition of philosophy which was imported into England in the middle 1930s and hailed almost as a new religion (certainly as a new 'faith' and way of life), reason, and the knowledge and understanding to which it was applied, has tended to be interpreted in a special and restricted way. The focus has tended to be on detached ratiocinative thinking, rather than thinking as a function of the whole person in investigative action moved by feeling and vital interest. Reason, practical and theoretical, desire, emotion, cognition, tend to be reified, and as reified, to be considered in relation to one another externally rather than as organic parts of a single complex functioning whole. In the volume mentioned, *Reason,* this analytic atomizing tendency is well offset in a number of the individual papers, particularly in Ryle's 'A rational animal', Max Black's paper 'Reasonableness' and Edgley's 'Practical reason'. But the general tendency remains, all the same.

Not much interest, either, had been shown in the aesthetic, the arts and art education, among philosophers of education. Exceptions are R.K. Elliott, John White, David Aspin, myself, and, from 'pure' philosophy, Ronald Hepburn. This neglect is a pity, as the arts, usually under the weather, are more so than ever at the present time—and at this same present time could prove themselves of special importance in an age of increased 'leisure'.

3. The aesthetic as a model for educative learning

Apart from the special importance of education in the arts, to which I shall return shortly, I want at this point to suggest that the aesthetic is a very good model for educative learning in any subject of the curriculum. This may at first sight seem to be an expression of bias towards the aesthetic and the arts. But I think it can be shown that 'aesthetic', even as conventionally defined by aestheticians, has a much wider application than to objects of the senses and works of art. A very generally accepted account of 'aesthetic' is that when *anything* (often, but not necessarily, a sense object) is attended to 'for its own sake', or for itself, and is sufficiently interesting to hold our attention, that 'anything' becomes an aesthetic object. We are not primarily interested in it because it increases our knowledge about things, or because it is useful, or because it has economic value, or for any extraneous reason or cause, but because it is itself, and holds our attention and gives us a certain joy in the actively attentive contemplation of it. The joy, aesthetic joy, arises out of our intensely active (yet contemplative) interest in the complex forms and qualities of the object, and notably in its form, a unity of complexity which comes, as we attend to it, to be seen intuitively as an inherently interesting many-in-one. It is very important to keep in mind this attention to the forms and qualities of the object, for the aesthetic joy arises out of this attention to them and is not something self-centred which can be cultivated as an isolated feeling on its own.

It is important, too, to be clear about the stipulations that, in the aesthetic as such, extraneous values, increase of knowledge-about, economic or use-value are not intrinsically relevant to the definition of the aesthetic. But aesthetic experience may be related, intrinsically or extrinsically, to cognition in other senses, or have use or economic value. Having had aesthetic experience of an art work of course increases our knowledge *about* it. Again, a beautiful pot made by a craftsman-artist not only has use-value, but the aesthetic enjoyment of it extends to the handling and efficient using of it. Its usefulness here is distinguishable from the aesthetic joy in its form, and yet its handling qualities are part of its aesthetic form, and the joy of handling is an aesthetic experience.

Pure aesthetic experience is a concrete delight, concentrated on the form of the object apprehended. In terms of my earlier account of feeling as immediate indwelling experience, aesthetic experience when it is positive, has positively toned affect of feeling (IA-O) which is cognitively-affective perception of form. It is not a static reflection, or duplication of form, but an actively vital process of grasping that form, an indivisibly cognitive-affective grasping of it, and in process of grasping it coming to appreciate the form more fully. This is pure aesthetic apprehension as such: and it is an autonomous and self-contained experience, complete in itself, or perhaps inspiring the creation of a work of art also autonomous and self-contained. But there are delights in form which are, qua their aesthetic character, equally self-sufficient and enjoyed for their own sake, and yet also organic aspects of knowledge and understanding in other and wider senses. One familiar example of this is the aesthetic joy of pure mathematics. Polanyi remarks that the joy of mathematics is purely aesthetic.[6] An elegant argument in theoretical or empirical science, or in philosophy, can equally have aesthetic quality, and yield aesthetic pleasure in that quality. But it would not be true to say that, as in the purely aesthetic or the aesthetic in the arts, the aesthetic pleasure is purely self-contained and ends in autonomous self-containment. The purposes and motives in pursuing mathematics, scientific investigation, philosophy, are not simply aesthetic enjoyment, though they contain it when being pursued with vital interest. The aesthetic enjoyment is an inherent part of the assiduous pursuit, but the ultimate aim and motive is better knowledge and understanding (largely knowledge- and understanding-that) of their objective subject matters.

The knowledge and understanding of mathematics, science and philosophy is constrained—in different ways—by the independent forms and structures of their subject matters, which are to be understood conceptually, as the pure aesthetic and the arts are not. Perhaps pure mathematics is nearer to the pure aesthetic than the others because mathematics, being non-empirical, concentrates aesthetic delight on the form of pure logical constructions. But mathematics is still constrained by the independent nature of logic. A 'beautiful' theorem must conform to a logic which is independent of it. For science and philosophy it is the facts of an independent experienced world which constrain the forms of their cognitive constructions.

This, I think, applies generally to all 'subjects' in the curriculum, though I am certainly not competent to expound how, in different ways, it does apply to them all. It will be clear that I am not arguing that all knowledge and understanding is 'aesthetic', but that what I am calling aesthetic interest and joy is an intrinsic part of the enterprise of educative learning of any 'subject' or area of what is sometimes called 'cognitive' knowledge. Searching after and coming to understand *form* is the most fundamental motive of all knowledge-seeking. We are faced everywhere with bits of information or experience which may seem to be disconnected, often chaotic and yet, we may darkly suspect, have connections and forms uniting them which we do not as yet understand, yet may desire to. The desire to find relationships, order, form in what is puzzling and challenging is certainly one of the deepest drives of human beings. It is not simply that we add more to our stock of conceptual or empirical knowledge, count up the more that we have come to know and understand, though that has its satisfactions. It is not something which can be adequately tested by examinations or other assessments. It is, when genuine, a total kind of experience of personal life and a manifestation of a holistic personal development, a development of imagination, feeling, emotion, will, courage which can overcome the frustrations of apparent defeat. Disciplined following of this urge is an essential part of the life of personal mind in any sphere of knowledge.

Another aspect of this emphasis on holistic personal understanding is shown in an article by Professor J. Passmore, on 'Teaching to be critical'.[7] Passmore suggests that in calling a person 'critical' one is asking what kind of a *person* he/she is. This is partly though not fully worked out in his paper.

Teaching a child to be critical is, clearly, not telling him/her things, imparting facts. Nor is it a habit, though there are habitual ingredients in every skill. And if being critical is a skill, it does not consist in being able to state how to solve a problem but in being able to solve it. It is, however, more than a skill: it might be called a 'character trait'.

> To call a person 'critical' is to characterise him, to describe his nature, in a sense in which to describe him simply, as 'capable of analysing certain kinds of fallacy' is not to describe his nature. It is a natural answer to the question 'What kind of a person is he?' to reply 'Very critical', when it would not be a natural answer that the person in question is a skilful driver.[8]

Furthermore, whereas skills may be relatively easy to teach, it is far more difficult, because being critical is a character trait, to teach criticism. 'A critical person, in this sense, must possess initiative, independence, courage, imagination, of a kind which may be completely absent in, let us say, the skilful critic of the performance oɩ a laboratory technician.'[9] 'Critical thinking as it is exhibited in the great traditions conjoins imagination and criticism in a single form of thinking; in literature, science, history, philosophy or technology the free flow of imagination is controlled by criticism, and criticisms are transferred into a new way of looking at things.'[10] This is not just natural ability predeterminedly operating automatically. It is, one must stress, personal and individual *engagement*. It is thinking, feeling, being interested, active questioning and testing out so that understanding and knowing become *possessed* by the person. Discussion may of course sometimes find fault: but its positive function is discriminating understanding.

Passmore is commenting on what it means to be a 'critical person', perhaps in a sense in which the use of such a term applies to a person who is critical in a marked degree. More broadly, being critical characterizes *all* intelligent learning and understanding—apart from learning pure skills, or mere assimilation of established facts, in so far as these can be separated at all from the rest. It applies to the learning of science, philosophy, history, geography, and to the knowledge and understanding of values in art, morals, personal understanding. Being critical is one aspect of 'getting the feel' of the relationships in any subject or theme or enterprise; conversely, 'getting the feel of', 'feeling into', any of these is a condition of relevant critical understanding. In other words the person learning has to become involved as a person. And this is an *occurrent* process, of coming to know and understand, and, perhaps, of 'becoming educated'.

As I have just said, this applies, though in different ways and with different stresses, to learning and becoming educated in anything, or acquiring educated understanding of anything. In this book, however, we have been particularly concerned with the experience and understanding in spheres of value, artistic, moral, personal. I now want to comment on these individually.

4. 'Religious education'

There is religion, and religious education, too. In this book I have not discussed religion. I have done so in other books and articles—in *Ways of Knowledge and Experience* on religion generally and Christianity in particular, in *Preface to Faith* and in *The Rediscovery of Belief*,[11] on Christian religion and its theology. I cannot return to that (or advance on it) here. I can only offer a few opinions, without defending them by argument, and must do so now because I believe it would be irresponsible simply to leave out any consideration of a topic of such immense importance in our historical cultures, in personal life and education. I am acutely, embarrassingly, aware that this is a subject of immense complexity on which whole libraries of books have been written, that it is as controversial as it is complex, and wholly impossible to 'deal with' in a page or two.

I think that some basic teachings on religion, and religions, should be part of any core curriculum in schools—and, because of the need for brevity now, I have here in mind only the common schools and not those with specific religious foundations.

It seems to me obvious that children should learn, to start with, that there are important things in the world called 'religion' and 'religions', and monstrous that this should be left out of their knowledge of sheer fact. And if there are—as there are—great dangers of the wrong sort of dogmatic indoctrination in the teaching of religion, there is, equally, an implied wrong sort of negative dogmatic indoctrination on the part of those who (perhaps without any real understanding of religion) personally 'have no use' for religion, and would leave religion out of education. Children should certainly know that there is religion and that there are religions, and they should be taught at least some minimum about religion and religions. I use the plural because we live in pluralistic societies, where there are a number of religions, each making its own claims. But I hasten to add that this does not imply the shallow and pretentious claim that children (particularly younger children) should embark on 'the comparative study of religions'. The recognition that there are at least several 'higher' religions is important, as is the respect for sincere differences in belief. This recognition, and perhaps respect and tolerance, can be encouraged if children are invited to visit—say in a community where there has been a substantial incursion of Muslim immigrants—mosques where religious worship is actually taking place. This is in fact being practised in some communities.

That is, so far, only saying that children should be aware of the fact that religion and religions exist, and that they are important to those who believe in them.

In this country, until the wave of immigration greatly increased in size, 'religious education' has, more or less, meant 'Christian-religious-education'. I cannot here comment on the ways Christian-religious-education has actually been taught, and mistaught, in schools. I can only repeat that, in this century, there has been an immense volume of writing on the subject, and that, in my opinion, the intelligent study of religious education has shown a tremendous development of understanding of how religion should, and should *not*, be taught. I cannot estimate how widely this good influence extends. My impression is that it has been very considerable, but that there are still very large pockets of resistance—and not only from 'fundamentalists'. In my own experience, I know of many, many people who have been 'put off' for life from any enlightened consideration of religion, and particularly of what they think is 'Christian religion', by the way in which they have been indoctrinated as children into beliefs which, as they grew older, they have found impossible honestly to sustain.

Religion does, and must, affirm or presuppose beliefs, beliefs which in *some* sense claim to be true. In Christianity some of these beliefs are stated in creeds (for example the Apostles' Creed), assent to some of which is almost a condition of being called a 'Christian'—in the sense of rightfully belonging to the body of Christians. There are some exceptions to this—for instance, the Quakers. But what kind of 'claims to truth' are they? In some, though not all, of the higher religions they include affirmations of a transcendent Being, variously categorized, usually called 'God'. For the theistic believer 'God' somehow, in some manner beyond human comprehension and language, 'exists'. (Though 'beyond language', there are huge libraries of metaphorical and analogical religious language!) This is the firm belief on which those who hold the belief will stake their existence and base their whole lives. But we also know that for the proposition 'God exists' there are no unchallengeable proofs, though there have recently been interesting philosophical attempts to state the traditional 'proofs' in new and rationally persuasive ways. But even with full recognition of the analogical character of all statements about God, it is impossible to affirm that we have true, clear, conceptual *Knowledge* (capital K) about God. Beliefs are, in the wide sense in which I have used the word, 'cognitive'. But honest faith must always have an agnostic element.

There is, however, another approach to religious knowledge, from the side of religious experience. The relevance of this approach is suggested by the etymology of the word 'religion'—re-ligare, ligare, to bind. Professor P.H. Hirst writes very succinctly on this approach.

> Religious statements are attempts to talk intelligibly about certain aspects of man's natural experience, his experience in everyday contexts not simply in such specifically religious contexts as say church worship. The view is that religious discourse picks out man's awareness that the universe is not self-explanatory, that human experience and knowledge are set in ultimate mystery and that this awareness breaks in on man in a great variety of circumstances. Some such experience we have come to call numinous, others we regard as more mystical in character. Religious language is then regarded not as telling us facts about the inner nature of the mystery, but as attempts in

parabolic or metaphysical language to relate and make intelligible these experiences. The only language we have is language whose meaning is closely tied to our experience of the finite world. When it comes to understanding this area of mystery and to answer limiting questions about our experience of it, then our language becomes figurative. Most developed religions for instance have come to speak of experience of mystery as experiences of a 'person' but this is simply an analogy or picture by which to characterise the experiences.

When it comes to tests for the truth of religious statements, the point must be the adequacy of the pictures in making sense of the range and circumstances of the experiences.[12]

I very fully agree with this, and in stressing the 'breaking in' element, I think I would emphasize more the quite extraordinary effect that this impingement, *ex gratia*, a kind of 'grace', can have on the whole being of a person and on the totality of his/her affective and conative response. It is not just that the universe is an insoluble puzzle. It is all that, certainly! But it is the complex impact of, and the complex response to, the *Mysterium Tremendum* which is so total and so profoundly moving. It is a kind of 'knowing' through envelopment in a 'Cloud of Unknowing'. For the unknown author of the work of this title who appears to be a man trained in all the complexities of theology, it was a temporary casting aside of all *that* kind of 'knowing'. And for him, at those moments of ecstasy, it was certainly a non-propositional knowing. 'By love may he be gotten and holden; but by thought never.' Or Tennyson: 'Closer is He than breathing, and nearer than hands and feet.' Here is a claim not to truth of statement nor, I think, only to authenticity, but also to validity of experience. These men's perspectives were Christian; but of course it need not be that.

This stress on religious experience suggests at least one way in which religious education might be approached in schools. I hardly think religion can be taught in the sense that other subjects may be taught. But some of its quality can be learned from the impact of the integrity of a sensitive religious teacher. One affiliation of the word 'education' (*educare*) is with 'nourishment'. Good religious education ought at least to include some spiritual nourishment for personal life. However that be, there seems to be one inviolable rule of religious teaching—that children should never feel externally forced into religious commitment, nor to unwilling engagement in religion which presupposes such required commitment. An elementary principle of any 'grammar of assent' is that assent must be given in authentic freedom.

All this is general and intentionally so. And the last paragraph but one describes a quality of religion which is attainable only in developed and intelligent maturity. This in itself is significant in any discussion of religion, for there is a sense in which any deep understanding experience of religion can only come with maturity and intelligence. Religion in one aspect of it is a childlike thing, and for young children, one way or another, it has to be childlike. But when understanding and experience of religion does not mature with the growth of intelligence, it becomes, or remains, *childish*. Childish religion in adults can be, often is and has been, a great menace, and childish fundamentalism in adults which *will* not, which does not *want*, to think, is a menace which can do far more harm than good. (How much hideous cruelty, torture, wars, mass murdering, religious fanaticism has engendered and goes on daily engendering, is beyond human imagination or calculation.)

If religion in depth, for those who do not simply dismiss it, requires maturity and intelligence of understanding as well as feeling, what kind of teachers are required for religious education, and what can they *do* in the classroom, where both younger and older children are concerned? Once again, much has been, and is being written about this, and I can only record an observation or two. I think no subject is more difficult to teach well.

Suppose, for the nonce, it is in the Christian context that religion is being 'taught'. Teachers here *must* be trained and well-equipped in the basics of the theology of Jewish-Christian religion, and in the basics of Biblical-historical criticism. This does not, of course, mean that they directly teach these things—clearly utterly beyond the comprehension of young children—though some of it to some extent comprehensible to maturer adolescents. But equipped with such background knowledge and having assimilated it, teachers can sometimes use it in explaining things which puzzle young minds. Without such equipment they cannot be competent teachers. Without it they cannot even begin to cope with the devastatingly seemingly-simple, but profoundly metaphysical questions children ask, as: Was Jesus a man? Or was he God? How could he be both? Was he just the 'Son' of God? What does that mean? Are we supposed to worship God, or Jesus? . . . Or, 'Did he do miracles? Did he really rise from the dead? Are these just stories, or are they true? . . .

These are real puzzles, not only for children in the classroom. They, and hundreds of others like them, go on puzzling (among those who remain interested) through the generations. They are historico-theological problems, and in the Jewish-Christian tradition they are unavoidable, because this religion is a theologically saturated religion.

But though this is true, there is another side. Religion is certainly not to be simply identified with theology, and only those who happen to be interested in these historico-theological questions need pursue their metaphysics. The spirit of a religion is *distinguishable* from its theology. Sometimes it is said of Christianity that its ethics can be taught apart from its religion. This is arguable, but if historical Christianity is an overstatement, and even if the word 'theology' is substituted for 'religion', it is still not quite true—for the reasons given. But it *is* true that what counts most in any religion is not its metaphysical theology, but its spirit. And, in fact, the spirit of Christian ethics, with its teaching of love rather than law, has influenced and has been accepted by a vastly greater number of people than those who call themselves 'Christian' or accept Christian orthodox theology. And it is this spirit it seems to me, which should be stressed if the teaching of religion in school is carried out in the Christian context.

If so, the spirit is best learned, not by talking *about* Christian religion (or much about its theology), but by presenting its spirit as expressed by the great religious teachers and prophets themselves. The Bible—Old and New Testaments—is a rich mine of such teaching. Here again teachers have to be *au fait* with the structure of the Bible, its history, how it came to be written, the contexts of its different books, the relation between, and the contrast between, the Old Testament and the New. Good teachers will know where to find what they need for their particular purposes-here-and-now: and they will use the different translations, which like maps, are made with different purposes in mind. The Authorized Version, with its glorious range of language adapted for different purposes—simple and elegant story-telling, the impressive rhetoric of the Psalms and Minor and Major prophets, the parables of the Gospels, the variety of styles within the Epistles—all these can convey the feeling of the religion and the moral values they express, in a way ordinary talk about religion cannot. For other purposes, other translations are often needed. For the understanding of the meaning of Corinthians XIII, for instance, Moffatt's translation is illuminating. For the Authorized Version's 'Charity thinketh no evil', Moffatt's 'Love is never glad when others go wrong' gives fuller meaning. And so on.

The main point here is, I think, that though the scriptures were not written (or translated) consciously as 'art for art's sake', they *are* art. And as literary art they do not appeal as abstractions, but as expressive embodiment of religious and moral life and meaning. Thus they communicate as some other ways cannot, because of their wholeness.

5. Moral education

On moral education I wish only to refer to and very briefly comment on two writers, John Wilson and Gilbert Ryle.

Wilson's Farmington Trust research work produced and stimulated a lot of writing.[13] He recommends that one or two periods a week be given over to the teaching of morality, with material provided for teachers which would summarize the concepts, procedures, kinds of reasoning, and the abilities presupposed in the study of morality. The material for teachers would not be philosophy, but methodology. Rather than setting out to discuss particular moral issues, it would take simple examples, would try to show that there are right and wrong, rational and irrational ways of making up one's mind on moral matters. Morality, it is argued, has its own methodology: it should be taught on its own, just as principles of arithmetic are taught. This procedure would be a good way of preparing for the time when real moral problems have to be met and real decisions taken.

I agree about the definite need for explicit moral teaching in school and for definite periods to be devoted to it. It is true that moral questions may come into any lesson, and that the school itself is up to a point a moral mentor. But the subject is far too serious to be left to chance as it very often is. I remember after the war meeting a group of Japanese teachers who came to London to discuss the problems of moral re-education in Japanese schools. We were, I think, at that time much too superior about it. 'Of course', we said, '*we* don't have special periods for moral instruction (or education). It just comes in.'

That may have gone quite a long way a hundred years ago. It was not enough forty years ago, and it is certainly not enough now. Moral education *may* have 'gone down' successfully in some schools in earlier days when there was a fair body of generally accepted values, and the generation gap was marked in quite different ways. Our conceptions of values today are uncertain, fluid to a degree not known several generations ago. They cannot be taken for granted; they have to be rediscovered and re-established freshly and in new idioms. Traditional authority is questioned. There is—it comes to our hearing and seeing daily—a horrifying spectacle of violence, cruelty, race hatred and persecution, trafficking in drugs . . . pollution, the wastage of natural resources . . . Young people are brought face to face in life and through the media with these and much more. What they think and feel about them, and about sex, truthfulness, honesty, consideration of others, will of course depend crucially upon the kind of parents they have and the atmosphere of the family in which they live, the schools they go to. They are lucky if they have intelligent and responsible parents; statistically, this luck is said to extend to less than half the population. As children quite desperately need help and guidance in the sorting out of their moral tangles, confusions, conflicts, what could be more urgent than that they should be given the chance to talk freely and without inhibition among their peers and under an older, wiser person of experience specially trained to help them?

But is what they desperately need help in, the learning of *procedures*? To say that this is what they chiefly need seems to be a very odd sort of answer. Certainly any mature person having to take moral decisions, employs, must employ, procedures in thinking and deciding what they are going to do. And in a sense it is true that morality is a 'form of thought' in its own right, and that 'there are serious and non-serious ways of making up one's mind on moral issues'. But it is artificial, and impossible, to isolate these procedures from the whole of the rest of the process of a person's deciding and acting responsibly in those particular circumstances. There are of course the routine duties which are often carried out almost automatically and without needing much thought. But actions which are the result of the deliberation of a character with developed sentiments are—as I tried to show in Chapter VII—expressions of a holistic attitude and cannot be captured in purely intellectual or conceptual terms. The comparison between the teaching of moral procedures and the teaching of arithmetic is quite misleading. Arithmetic does not contain an empirical constituent as moral thinking does. Its calculations are not like deliberations about what to do in a life situation. Arithmetic is a rule-governed activity and its rules determined by the nature of agreed symbols used logically. One can begin to learn arithmetic with a clean slate. One cannot get near moral procedures, or even know what they might mean, without a long trail of the experience of values, without an already built-in sense and feeling that some things are more important than others and that it somehow matters what we choose to do.

Teaching moral procedures as such, would not, I think, be moral education, though such teaching might well be a section within moral education. We may agree that moral thinking about procedures has its own forms and has to be learned. But it is *moral thinking* only as it is motivated morally, its form reflecting the built-up motives, sentiments, character, judgement and feeling of a moral agent. Short of this, the learning of procedures would be more like being trained in formal techniques and skills than like moral education. Significant moral decision calls forth the organized capacities of a person, rational but more than rational. Or, if the term is preferred, it is a holistic rationality.

Gilbert Ryle has some telling things to say about moral education in his paper 'Can virtue be taught?'[14] He observes:

> Arithmetic can be taught, and there are professional teachers of it. So can skills be taught—but through coaching and practice rather than just being told. Again, in matters of morals, as in skills and arts, we learn first by being shown by others, then by being trained by others, naturally with some worded homily, praise and rebuke, and lastly by being trained by ourselves. But we don't teach people to be *honest* by training them in competence and efficiency in skills. It happens (if it happens) in a different way. Conscientiousness is not part of dexterity, of any kind (even of thinking). We have to learn to feel, to care, to come to recognise for ourselves that some things are of intrinsic *importance*.
>
> Can one be taught to feel things that one would not otherwise have felt? Yes, in a familiar sense of 'taught', we can. Separated off from all considerations about acquiring information and acquiring proficiencies, we were 'taught' by our parents—by their tones of voice, underlining the positiveness of concern for some things, the distaste for others, and the difference between the gravity of some offences and the lesser gravity of others. We were taught to care more whether we had cheated or not than whether we had won the game or lost it, to care much more whether we were hurting the old dame's feelings than whether we were being badly bored at her little tea-party, and so on. Of course all this can be called 'just conditioning': your now feeling shocked by what used to shock your father or headmaster is just another effect of suggestion.[15]
>
> Why do we resist accepting in theory what we accept unhesitatingly in daily life? Why are we reluctant to accept in theory 'that people can be properly said to learn to want things, learn to admire things, learn to care about things, learn to treat things seriously in word, deed and tone of voice, learn to be revolted by things, learn to respect, approve and back things, learn to scorn and oppose things and so on?[16]

Now comes the central point—and it is the same point I have been trying to make from the first sentence of this book.

> One source is this. In our abstract theorising about human nature we are still in the archaic habit of treating ourselves and all other human beings as animated department stores, in which the intellect is one department, the will is another department and the feelings a third department. Our poor bodies, of course, are not departments but basement kitchens, sewers or at best shop windows. So we take it for granted that as the intellect is notoriously the one

department into which lessons go, our wills and feelings are not themselves teachable. They cannot know anything; they cannot be more or less cultured or cultivated ... Somehow or other our intellects can indeed harness, drive, steer, flog, coax, goad and curb our wills and our feelings; but in themselves these two brainless faculties are in the civilized man just what they are in the savage; there is no schooling of them.

This department store yarn is sheer fairy story. It answers to almost nothing in the actual composition of human nature. Try to think for a minute of some friend of yours in terms of it; try to describe his actions and reactions during some recent crisis in terms borrowed from it, and you will see that a description which fits the department store yarn cannot be made to apply to your friend, and a description which fits your friend's behaviour cannot be wrenched into tallying with the department store yarn. No novelist, dramatist or biographer nowadays dreams of depicting his heroine or even his villain in department store terms.[17]

I will not apologize for quoting Ryle at such length, for it is a brilliant epitome by an 'analytical' philosopher of a vital synthesis which I, from a rather different background, hold to be absolutely central to the understanding of education generally and moral education in particular. It is the insight into the indivisible unity of the make-up of the complex human person. Only thinking beings can feel and act morally. And only thinking beings who can feel morally, can think and act morally. I think Ryle might have been sympathetic to what I have called the 'areteic' emphasis, and the 'style' of life in which it is expressed. If there is moral knowing, it is, on one side, knowing through being and action expressive of being. It is in this way that the importance of the *content* of morality (the teaching of which is so belittled by some contemporary writers) can be learned and come to be possessed.

6. The arts and aesthetic education

(a) *The aesthetic and arts education*

All that has been said about feeling and wholeness applies, and perhaps even more amply, to the arts and art education. For in morals and moral education, sense perception and feeling for, and of, meaning through perception do not figure directly—though of course it is always true that the instrument of willing, feeling and thinking is an embodied person. But in the arts, as I have been saying all along, the body plays a particularly important part. We listen to, or play, music: without concentrated psychophysical attention to the music there is no musical experience. (I referred earlier to Menhuin's remarks in his master-class on the importance, in the awareness of music, of bodily postures and movements.) Dance is perhaps the most obvious illustration of bodily expression of meaning, meaning which can only be understood and known, in one way to the dancers, in another way to the spectators, through aesthetic perception of the movements of dance. In the action and speech of drama, in the sounds and rhythms of poetry read aloud or imagined as read, dramatic and poetic meaning are first apprehended, in that all the arts first impinge upon the senses. Pictures and sculptures have to be seen and looked at—and this is not only a matter of seeing with the eyes but of responding, sometimes very evidently, in subconscious bodily movements.

The novel in literature may seem an exception to this emphasis on bodily perception. Here, the stress is on the transparency of words, where we imaginatively seem to see straight through to 'semiotic' meaning. This suggests that meaning-embodied is more a thing of imagination than of perceiving body. There is a valid point here, but it is only partially true. The sensible and formal qualities of style essentially are *vehicles* of imagination: the two are fused aesthetically, and it is this to which the term 'meaning-embodied' properly applies.

If all this is true, we come back to Ryle's demolition of the foolish myth of our human nature as an animated department store, with the intellect as the one department through which we can learn, with feelings that 'cannot know anything, cannot be more or less cultured or cultivated . . .' Logic, mathematics, science and much other factual knowledge we can acquire largely through intellect and intellectual intuitions—though, as we have seen, mental feelings have their part to play in motivation and enjoyment—and sometimes aesthetic feelings. The same is true, though to a more limited extent, of moral knowledge and procedures. But the *first* approach to actual works of art, which are always particular and individual objects of perception, cannot, as aesthetic, be 'intellectual' or 'conceptual'. We cannot come to know and understand works of art first from the top of the head, and then downwards. Experience, feeling, direct, particular, concrete, comes first; intellectual analysis, perhaps later. This may sound artificial and divisive if the word 'concrete' is not stressed. For of course experience, as concrete, is charged even as perception with implicit concepts of many kinds. If it is a 'gut' reaction as it at first often is, it is the gut reaction of an embodied person who is an organic indivisible whole, and who can go on in many ways to reflect on his/her experience and the objects of that experience.

If we accept this as true, and remember at the same time the profound influence of the 'fairy story' of the divided department-store human person, it is easy to see why, among a number of other causes, education in the arts is assumed to have such a low priority claim for a place on the school curriculum.

I think that this 'low priority' applies to *all* the arts, considered as art qua art. (There are of course exceptions: in some schools this is not true.) In 'all the arts' are included here English literature, its prose and poetry, drama, music, dance, the visual arts, film/television. But though this inclusiveness of use of the word 'art' is perfectly justified and needs no defence, it is a fact of common experience that when we talk of 'art', or of 'art education' we often think only of the visual arts. In government and other reports which include reference to 'art education' it is usually assumed that this refers to the visual arts. If the topic being discussed were music, or dance, or music education or dance education, it would not be customary to refer to education in these as 'art education', though of course in fact music and dance are, equally, 'arts' in their own right. A curiously significant anomaly arises over English literature. In current (and controversial) discussion of the 'core curriculum', it seems to be always assumed that what is dubbed 'Eng. lang. and lit.' must be an essential part of the core curriculum. The aspersion of 'low priority' does not apply here. Why is this? I think it arises partly out of the nature of the 'subject' English literature, and partly out of assumptions behind the jargon 'Eng. lang. and lit.' Literature, I think everyone would agree, is 'about life'; and literature a prime means of extension of our knowledge about human life. It would be difficult to find reasonable objections to this as a function of education: and virtually to *stop* there is to escape awkward questions about this thing called 'art'. Many people who take for granted that English literature must be a 'core' subject do stop there. But this is half-baked (or even unbaked or raw) ignorance of what literature is. Literature informs about human nature, morals, society, sometimes ideology, 'life', the condition of man . . . certainly. But it is as art that literature, and particularly great literature, properly does so. Or rather, it does not so much 'inform about' as give direct insight into life's meanings. Teaching English literature without attention to it as art is, where it happens, again half-baked. So there is a complex tension in literature teaching, between emphasis on subject matter, and art. I need not repeat here what I have said throughout about embodiment of meaning in art. I will only make the rather obvious comment that the life-subject-matter which is an intrinsic part of literature, is life as seen and understood and expressed by the artist (with whom we share it) in terms of his/her linguistic medium, and *that*, at certain stages of teaching literature, must be attended to. This may help to bring out its significance as *embodied content*, as distinct from its being a mere mirroring of subject matter. Perhaps the other reason why literature slips easily into the core curriculum without consideration of it as art, is hidden in the coupling jargon 'lang. and lit.' Everyone agrees about the appalling inability of many pupils at the end of school life to string a sentence together, and that teaching of 'lang.' needs boosting. In the coupling, 'lit.' slips in easily too.

I have headed this section 'The arts and aesthetic education'. It calls for a brief comment. Art is, internally, aesthetically apprehended through and through: but the aesthetic is not identical with art, and there is more in art than its essentially aesthetic factor—in some arts its subject matter, in all art its embodied content. And the aesthetic is of course not confined within the arts. If the aesthetic is contemplative enjoyment of *anything* worth holding the attention and without the entry, in the actual experience, of extraneous motives, then its range is wide indeed, as I have indicated earlier in the chapter. It includes, too, all the multifarious delights of natural phenomena everywhere. Rupert Brooke, in 'The Great Lover', enumerates some of the *sensuous* joys of ordinary life:

> These have I loved:
> > White plates and cups, clean-gleaming,
> Ringed with blue lines; and feathery, faery dust;
> Wet roofs, beneath the lamp-light; the strong crust
> Of friendly bread; and many-tasting food;
> And radiant raindrops couching in cool flowers;
> And flowers themselves, that sway through sunny hours,
> Dreaming of moths that drink them under the moon;
> Then, the cool kindliness of sheets, that soon
> Smooth away trouble; and the rough male kiss
> Of blankets; grainy wood; live hair that is
> Shining and free; blue-massing clouds; the keen
> Unpassioned beauty of a great machine . . .

The enjoyment of all these things is good in itself: and a life that is full of it is a life full of unlimited potential delights, so that an ageing man, Thomas Hardy, looking back, as if when life has ended, can write in his poem 'Afterwards':

When the Present has latched its postern behind my tremulous stay,
    And the May month flaps its glad green leaves like wings,
Delicate-filmed as new-spun silk, will the neighbours say,
    'He was a man who used to notice such things'?

If it be in the dusk when, like an eyelid's soundless blink,
    The dewfall-hawk comes crossing the shades to alight
Upon the wind-warped upland thorn, a gazer may think,
    'To him this must have been a familiar sight'.

.   .   .   .   .

If, when hearing that I have been stilled at last, they stand at the door,
    Watching the full-starred heavens that winter sees,
Will this thought rise on those who will meet my face no more,
    'He was one who had an eye for such mysteries'?

The 'education' of children 'to notice such things' cannot be a formal thing, with rules, but must be rather a sympathetic encouragement by parents and teachers as much by their own attitudes and 'noticing' interests, as anything else. In the daily bringing up, at home and at school, it is often sadly lacking. But where it is present it is an initiation into what here in this context it may sound a little pompous to call 'aesthetic education'.

Education in the arts can do much to develop this 'noticing'.

(b) Visual art education in the curriculum

But education in the *arts* is indeed a serious and difficult challenge to education, and of course an immensely complex one, even if it is only because of the multiplicity of the arts, each art setting its own characteristic problems of content and method. Here I can only touch on the content and teaching of one group—the visual arts. It is a pity that it has to be so confined, for the personal, social, and cultural significance of the arts (in the plural), and education in them, is so varied. Recent writings in this field are not only voluminous, but often of very high quality, particularly since the middle 1960s, when there was an upsurge of new academic studies and research in arts education, conferences and reports, more—or less—official. Writings, too, in arts, arts education and aesthetics journals, and in books, have been showing a new vitality. (In the footnote I can only indicate a specimen or two.*)

* There is the Gulbenkian Report, *The Arts in Schools: Principles, Practice and Provision*, ed. Ken Robinson (London: Gulbenkian Foundation, 1982), and the Gulbenkian-cum-Leverhulme, *The Arts in Higher Education*, ed. Ken Robinson (Guildford: Society for

But here my remarks must be confined to the visual arts: it is the visual arts as what happens in the 'art-room' which first comes into most people's minds when 'art education' is mentioned. As such it often receives a polite or condescending nod; at times scarcely that.

Sometimes this supercilious attitude on the part of authorities is due to basically instrumentalist views of education, and of art as a pleasant leisure-time pursuit, revealing sad ignorance of what art is or what it can do in the cultural lives of individual and social human beings. But art educationists themselves must bear some of the responsibility, for a lack of clear or systematic thinking, until very recently, about the nature, content, and methods of art education.

A great deal has been thought and written about the instrumental effects of what is called children's 'art-making' on their growth and development—particularly in younger children. It helps them to come to terms with the perceptual world. Drawing improves the quality of observation and understanding. It teaches children to analyse objects: drawing can be involved with understanding one's feelings about things; it can be a means of re-organizing ideas and responses, or of transforming them into new images. All this is very true and very important. Along with it can go spontaneity and joy of expression, altogether good; and anything that interferes with it, destructive.

But it seems a pity that all drawing, painting, potting, modelling . . . should, by habit and custom, be labelled automatically 'art', or 'child art', with public exhibitions of these, and sometimes competitions. Some of it will show some of the characteristics of art; a great deal will not, though it can have a charm and attraction all its own. To say this does not—very emphatically not—in any way denigrate such children's work. Nor does it in any way deny the continuity of personal development or an overlapping between the beginnings of art and activities which help a child to see the external world more clearly, to

---

Research into Higher Education, 1982). There is Keith Swanwick's *A Basis for Music Education* (Windsor: NFER-Nelson, 1979). The Department of Education and Science Assessment of Performance Unit produced *Aesthetic Development* (1983), which offered interesting reflections on art and art education, particularly in relation to the difficult question of assessment. *Educational Analysis* (Vol. 5, No. 2, 1983) and the books edited by Malcolm Ross (*The Arts and Personal Growth*, 1980, *The Development of Aesthetic Experience*, 1982, *The Arts: A Way of Knowing*, 1983, and *The Aesthetic in Education*, 1985. Oxford: Pergamon) contained penetrating essays covering the range of the arts. In late 1983 the National Association for Education in the Arts was formed and in 1984 Ken Robinson launched *Arts Express*. These are but indications of the new vitality in the face, alas, of economic devitalization.

adjust practically to the external world, to learn many more things about it which would simply be lacking without the definite explorative exercises of drawing, painting, modelling. Nor is denied the enjoyment of learning in this way and the aesthetic delight which may occur in the forms of things 'for their own sake'. Nevertheless it is important to keep in mind the conceptual *distinction* between the practical and theoretic effects of these activities, and the early beginnings of 'art' proper which, as such, is neither practical nor aiming at the increase of cognitive understanding in the ordinary sense of these words. Young children's art, by definition, is of course not mature or developed art, though some of it is art all the same. But art, whether called by that name or not, is autonomous, and a slow, long discipline in its own right, and there is, and has been, a danger that, through a looseness in the conception of 'art', the need for its intriguing disciplines be overlooked. It may well be that very young children are often best left alone (without the word 'art' being uttered?!), given suitable materials, to discover for themselves. Beyond that stage a more positive approach is called for.

Two articles in the *Journal of Art and Design Education* attempt to repair something of these confusions. One, 'Towards critical study in the primary school' (Richard T. Kelsall), the other, 'The structure and content of art teaching in the secondary school' (John Steers)[18] are accounts of the authors' researches in these fields. The conjunction, in the same number of the *Journal*, is significant. There has been very little *liaison* between art education in the two fields. In the secondary school they tend to start all over again from scratch, without information about what has gone before.

Kelsall[19] argues for a broader approach to the art-education curriculum than has hitherto prevailed.

> Many art educators in recent years have called for the inclusion of what may be conveniently described as the development of critical abilities in Art and Design education. Critical study, it is argued, should complement the present emphasis on 'expression' in visual arts teaching. Critical study would be characterised by the ability of pupils to make judgements on their own work, as well as that of others, and to do this within a knowledgeable historical and cultural frame of reference. What is called for is a strengthening of the educational role of galleries, museums and professional artists together with an acceptance of the idea that critical study is not something that can be popped into the curriculum during adolescent years, but which needs to be experienced by children throughout their art education experience in appropriate forms so that it may be developed and extended from the infant school stage onward.

Kelsall emphasizes the importance of language and its crucial part in the development of discriminating aesthetic perception.

> The prime intention was to give emphasis to talking about art works in the experimental lessons which would include adult art works and the pupils' own art works. It was assumed that developing and expanding the vocabulary available to individual pupils would commensurately alter their perceptual abilities and understandings. Consequently, in addition to examining the effects of the experimental teaching on children's responses to art works, I also wished to examine its effects on their artistic expression . . . the children's picture-making ability.

With the usual necessary research precautions, comparisons of the effects of the experimental teaching on aesthetic development with a control group showed that in the latter

> there were no significant differences between their mean scores at the pre- and post-test stage in any of the four main response areas tested; the perceptual, the affective, the literal, and the identificational. By contrast, the experimental groups showed a highly significant change in their responses at the post-test stage. This change may be summarized as follows: the most notable change was an increase in references in the perceptual area which was reciprocated by a decrease in references in the literal area. In other words, these children appeared to be giving more attention to the colours and shapes and other sensory aspects of the works and rather less attention to the subject matter at the post-test stage compared with the pre-test stage.

The author claims no finality for his research and makes positive suggestions for further work. But the results (and the examples given on page 56 of the article) are interesting and I think the sort of thing one would reasonably expect.

John Steers' paper,[20] appositely complementary to Kelsall's, is concerned with the structure and content of art teaching in the secondary school. He rightly insists that this does not imply a rigid system or rigidly prescribed teaching. The syllabus is presented only as an essential basis: the details and methods must be worked out by teachers themselves on the spot. His main purpose is to encourage a fresh perspective.

> The greater part of the work of the art department is concerned with the production of art objects of one kind or another and little allowance is made for the development of critical awareness or an understanding of the cultural heritage of this country or of mankind as a whole. There is little obvious sequence in art education generally, or specifically in the secondary school. At every stage there is a tendency to ask pupils to start again at the beginning and

to ignore previous hard won experience ... [It is] a confused subject area generally lacking in direction and purpose.

In contrast to this is the belief 'that there are fundamental art experiences that are equally valid at all stages of pupil development: the content does not differ, the level of understanding and depth of involvement does.' In the project handbook of the research, three independent elements which must coalesce in the production of all art work were described as the motivational element, the perceptual element and the element of technique. Perceptual elements, for instance, would include shape, colour, texture, form, tone.

(c) History of art in the curriculum

What about history of art?

There are several bad misconceptions about history of art and its relation to art education. One, overdominated by the limited conception of art education as simply encouraging children to make their own 'self-expressive' art objects, rejects art history as 'irrelevant'—except perhaps in so far as an example from art history can help in this piece of practical making. Examples are to be picked out from 'history' to help now. The assumption behind this is nonsense. Picking out an example from 'history' has nothing to do with history, or with the context in history of the example(s) chosen. It ignores the essentially chronological factor of history.

An opposite mistake lies in the thinking of history as *just* (or mainly) chronology. Chronology is of course an ineradicable factor in our conception of history; but clearly it is only one factor in the history of human enterprise. That learning history is just learning dates and periods and committing them to memory is a common image. There is no doubt that some teaching of art history has been not unlike that.

There is another, and much more considerable, objection to the teaching of history of art in schools (except perhaps for a few specialists who will take examinations in it as a 'subject'), an objection which tends to isolate it from the direct study of the practice and appreciation of art. It is that history of art is too difficult and technical—a study of styles, iconography, etc.—altogether too remote for ordinary school consumption. This is, as I say, a considerable objection, and if the teaching of art history were simply a watered down version of this advanced study, it would be a very strong objection.

Anthony Dyson, who writes illuminatingly on art history in schools, offers a practical counter to this objection. He seriously addresses himself to the problem of the devising of courses in primary schools and in the lower levels of secondary education which will enrich the learning of all pupils, the majority of whom will never aspire to examination success in the history of art. He discusses 'what may be achieved in an ordinary classroom with the aid of a pile of postcard reproductions and photographs, a few colour transparencies, and a collection of everyday objects.'[21]

> ... the contemplation of a group of Cubist portraits, however eloquently supported by a teacher's commentary, may mean little to pupils whose previous looking and questioning has left them unprepared for the difficult feat of perceptual gymnastics, and probably unsympathetic towards images for which there may be no niche in their interest and experience. The way towards the appreciation of such images may need to be paved by a thorough consideration of their animating principles. In the case of the Cubist portraits, one such principle might be that of distortion; and it is suggested that, long before a Cubist portrait can be comprehended *as a Cubist portrait*, the formal principle of distortion (among other important characteristics) will need to be appraised, explored and understood by pupils.[22]

And an important point for educative learning:

> What has become in this country the traditional structure for art-historical studies is likely to make far more sense to the pupil ultimately needing to adopt it if it has been approached from the standpoint of early and frequent looking with no necessity to learn and remember names, dates and locations. What is important, though, is that a *sense* of human shaping, of chronology, of location and of cultural inflection be gained—almost by contagion: a realisation that an art object is the work of human hand and mind, the evidence of a particular moment of history, the product of a certain geographical region and the expression of a culture.[23]

In teaching the time-element, one might compare 'a photograph of a greengrocer's stall with one of a Byzantine mosaic': or 'a Cubist head and a Renaissance portrait': or Wembley Stadium and the Roman Colosseum. Questions arising out of such comparison of artefacts of different periods might be: 'When might each item have been made? Recently? Long ago? About how long ago?' Or,

> ... if a poster advertising an early motor car were to be juxtaposed with a photograph of, say, Boccioni's sculpture 'Unique forms of Continuity in Space' (1913), something of the avant-garde nature of the chosen art objects

might more clearly be seen by pupils, and the bewilderment experienced by contemporaries could be sensed more deeply.[24]

Robert Hughes' *The Shock of the New* contains many examples of this kind.[25]

(d) History, and history of art

The too-exclusively-chronological image of history can, as we said, be very misleading. It is an image of lists and names, dates, chronological tables, of things belonging to a long-gone past, not of great interest except to those who have a penchant for poking into the past, a past cut off irrevocably from the present. But, though the fact that in the nature of things there is a sequence in time of before or after is of course undeniable, chronology, or the *recording* or chronicling of events, is only a necessary and convenient abstraction from the living thing, the course of human events, which is history.

There is what I think is a generally acceptable distinction between two different things with the same name, 'history'. There is the *concrete* history which is the sequential happening of human affairs *as they happen*, and *written* history which is, properly, the imaginative account of these happenings based on such evidences and records as remain to us. Both of these have to do with what may be called 'real' time, in Bergson's[26] language, *durée réelle*. Concrete history is *durée réelle* in the sense that it is the time of human happenings as they occurred. Written history tries to capture this imaginatively. Bergson's homely example of real time is the experience of raising your arm. This 'real time' is known directly by intuition in experience. However, when, as a physicist or a mathematician, you try to record and measure time, you have to draw a static diagram, a line with points P^1, P^2 . . . through which a body B is supposed to pass at time T^1 and T^2, etc. Bergson develops this in his metaphysics. The point is that the recording and measuring, though they may tell you something important, can be very misleading if they induce you to believe that in the diagram of the static line with points you can grasp the essence of time, which is the *movement and sequence* which you can only know in the intuition of direct experience.

The concrete 'history' of art is what actually happens in 'real' time, the lived time of the artists who actually participated in it. The *written* history of art tries to take us imaginatively into that life. (Gombrich's *The Story of Art* would be an example of this.) Such written history is sensitive to the sequence of events, and may sometimes use chronological devices and diagrams as an *aide-mémoire*. But its aim is to recapture *durée réelle* for the imagination.

There is, I think, a significant difference between ordinary political or social history, and the history of art, and one very important for art education. Concretely speaking, archaeological, political, social history belong to the *durée réelle* of the past. Written history, aiming at as true an imaginative account of the past as it can achieve, makes use of relics—a flint axehead, a broken shard, a suit of armour, an old manuscript— relics which remain now from the past. With the aid of these, written history constructs its pictures. The relics *can* be enjoyed, often aesthetically, as imagined parts of the picture. But the prime object of the historical exercise is not aesthetic as such, but, as far as possible, historical truth. Primarily, the relics are 'evidences', and their aesthetic value the added grace. In history of art it is rather different. We do not naturally think of the corpus of the works of art which have come down to us from the past as 'relics' (though in a sense they are relics; if physical, usually corroded by time). Again, they may be 'evidences'; but we do not think of them primarily as this. Baroque music, Durham Cathedral, Giotto's frescoes, Tintern Abbey . . . are presented to us, *now*, as art, architecture, poetry, and there is the focus of attention upon them, upon works of art as such. That is one, sure, irreducible aspect of our experience of them. But it is one aspect only, however important, and if it were all, our understanding and our fullest enjoyment of them would be strictly limited. For though they are here, now, they also belong to the past, and to the *durée réelle* of the past. And since art is not only a present aesthetic object, but humanly, intentionally, meaning-embodied, the imaginative recognition and understanding of the historical context of works of art, as in their *durée réelle*, is internal to their fuller appreciation.

In this fuller appreciation we do two distinguishable things at the same time, indivisibly. The sense of history, time, situation, sequence, is not cut off, divided, from our present direct contemplation. We see the content, present in its form and direct appeal: and we see it (if we have the knowledge and historical insight) as belonging to its period. Our better understanding comes from the union of the two things. Take the historical sense away, or suppose it absent altogether, and our artistic understanding is much impoverished. The relation between historical sense and fullest appreciation is not external (history being consigned to the past) but internal. Historical study and insight is not merely an addition of information; it is an intrinsic part of full enjoyment and understanding. As I have already suggested, a work of art is not merely an aesthetic object (though it is that): it is the expressive embodiment made by the artist, living in and necessarily conditioned by his/her period: in enjoying the art we are at the same time enjoying an art of that period—if we have acquired the insight to do so. And teaching the history of art well is inseparable from teaching the understanding enjoyment of art itself.

> Time present and time past
> Are both perhaps present in time future,
> And time future contained in time past.
>
> ('Burnt Norton', T.S. Eliot)

I am saying, then, that arts education, if it is to be given, and received, *as a serious study and as part of the core of a liberal education*, must contain three main elements. First, it must offer opportunities for practical explorative work in several arts media, with such technical or other help as required. Secondly, it must initiate into the critical appreciation of given works of art. Thirdly, and integral with this, is some study— appropriate to the different age ranges—of the history of art.

Education in the arts, more generally speaking, needs to be looked at in a broad perspective, as an integral part of basic liberal education, and not as a sort of extra amenity for some people and when time can be spared from it after attending to the more 'important' items in the curriculum (preparatory for qualifying examinations). One reason (or a cause) why the arts have been consigned to a kind of annexe (in the next street?) of Ryle's 'department store' is, once again, the disease of compartmentalism. And to some extent this is true within art education itself—the separating off of practical art-making from the much larger thing which art education should be. Art education ought to be seen holistically as an education in which making of art objects, criticism of them as well as critical appreciation of given works contemporary or historical—all appreciated in their settings—are brought together. If this is accepted *then* art education can be seen much more clearly and more widely as a major enterprise of the curriculum. But to achieve this does require a broader and more liberal education of the teachers of art—and of each art within the range of the arts, from which of course there has to be choice. I think, however, that English language and literature—as art—should be considered basic in the curriculum.

7. Summary and conclusion ‾

To sum up a long chapter. In it I have selected a few things to be said about education, relevant to the rest of what has been said in the book.

Noting, and rejecting as they deserve, behaviourist, instrumentalist, manipulative views of education, I turned to the education of conceptual understanding. In recent philosophical thinking about education, as well as in education itself, there has been a far too *exclusive* emphasis on the—unquestionably important—intellectual understanding and knowledge of facts. Critical understanding in depth is a function not of intellectual reason only, but of a devoted attention of the whole person—whether it be in the field of facts or of values. In the knowledge and understanding of value, the union of thinking and feeling is particularly intimate. In support of this I commented on religious, moral and aesthetic education, all properly parts of a core curriculum of any education calling itself 'liberal'.

Religious education should be regarded principally as a sympathetic introduction to religious facts, values and experiences which must be freely entered into. But, though religion has its childlike aspects, the profundities and complexities of religion, and especially Christianity, are beyond the capacities of young (and I think any school-age) children to understand in depth. Christianity, with its historico-theological-metaphysical puzzles and disputes is beyond the full understanding of any but a minority of specialist adults—and that itself is a most questionable claim! As for children, many of the 'simple' questions of children have no simple answer. So religious education in schools (it seems to me) can only be an initiation, with readings, carefully selected borrowings, from the great religious prophets, teachers, writers, who can best give the 'feel' of the quality, and the great seriousness, of religion. It goes without saying, of course, that only the good teachers, knowledgeable in this most difficult field, can judge when, how, and what to choose and to say to the particular age-group they are teaching.

Then followed a brief impression of a recent account of moral education, one which advocates (rightly) specific periods to be devoted to it. But in this research on moral education, valuable up to a point, there is little or no recognition of what is nowadays called 'the hidden curriculum'. In the obsession with concepts, procedures, types of moral reasoning, methodology, the researchers seem blind to what is a quite vital and indispensable, indeed central, factor in any real moral education—the sensitizing of the inner responses to good and evil, the fundamental motivations and the autonomous judgements of the whole person of the pupil. In this sensitizing process the unspoken influence of teachers themselves as persons of moral integrity can have quite incalculable effect. (Some of the observations in Chapter VI on 'asymmetrical' personal relations have a bearing on this, pages 77–9.)

The aesthetic, though it includes enjoyment of art, includes much more. But good art education will enhance not only discriminating enjoyment of the arts, but quicken and develop the aesthetic enjoyment of everything else.

Arts education, including of course literature studied as art, should illuminate the understanding and enjoyment of art in several ways. (This was enlarged upon in two earlier chapters.) Education in the visual arts has been too exclusively focused on one essential aspect of it—the practical making of art objects. (Even here there has been a sad lack of liaison between what is done in the primary and in the secondary schools.) Art education needs to be far more broadly conceived. From the early years it should develop—of course with sensitive regard for the different stages of children's development—critical and appreciative understanding, both of the children's own work, and of the given works of established artists. This, in turn, should be linked to the history of art, both as giving some idea and feeling for chronology, *and* for the 'timelessness' and, in a sense, the contemporaneity of all good art.

I began this book, as I have ended it, with particular concentration on the arts and art education. This is not, of course, because I think that knowledge and understanding of them is the whole of education, or a complete model for all educational learning. The experience of art is sui generis. Each kind of art, and each work of art yields, concretely speaking, quite individual insights. But there is one feature of artistic experience, its *aesthetic* character, which, as I indicated earlier in the chapter, can be enjoyed, in indefinitely wide extensions, in life outside the arts. This 'aesthetic' is absorbed attention to the interesting forms and other qualities of whatever is apprehended 'for itself' or 'for its own sake'. This distinguishes it from interests in things merely as a means to something else—for example, increase of factual knowledge, or practical use.

The aesthetic interest in works of art (in at any rate the traditional sense) is interest in *perceptual* objects, since all works of art are perceptual objects. The most familiar example of its extension to conceptual fields is probably pure mathematics: we talk of a 'beautiful' proof. And this is easily, often, and appropriately applied to the beauty, 'elegance' of form, of a scientific or philosophical argument, a piece of biological, historical exposition, perhaps to a piece of moral insight into good or right. For some, it includes the content of religious meditation. It is a joy of actively intuitive contemplation of sometimes great complexities as unified wholes. The 'beauty' of these things is not something hedonistically sought after (any more than it is in the creation of art). Rather it is the reward of absorbed attention to anything worth attending to.

The teacher who stimulates and encourages this engrossed engagement of pupils in whatever they are studying, is teaching educatively, and the outcome is educative learning. The aesthetic satisfaction it brings is the reward of the holistic approach to knowledge and understanding of many things of many kinds, the approach which it has been the purpose of this book to emphasize.

References

Chapter I: 'Knowledge', 'Language' and Personal Development

1. David Hume, *Enquiries Concerning Human Understanding* and *Enquiries Concerning the Principles of Morals*, ed. L.A. Selby-Bigge. Oxford: Oxford University Press, 1975, Part 3, section 12.
2. Peter Abbs, *Reclamations*. London: Heinemann, 1979, pp. 27–8.
3. Department of Education and Science, *A Language for Life* (The Bullock Report). HMSO, 1975.
4. Malcolm Ross, 'The predicament of the arts' in Malcolm Ross (ed.), *The Aesthetic Imperative. Curriculum Issues in Arts Education*, Vol. 2, Oxford: Pergamon, 1981, pp. 1–2.
5. Peter Abbs, op. cit., p. 55.
6. Ibid., p. 53.
7. Peter Geach, *Mental Acts, their Contents and their Objects*. London: Routledge & Kegan Paul, 1971, p. 23.
8. Charles Darwin, *Autobiography*, ed. Nora Barlow. London: Collins, 1958, pp. 138–9.
9. Quoted in Peter Abbs (ed.), *Autobiography in Education*. London: Heinemann Educational Books, 1974, p. 63.
10. Mary Stewart, *The Ivy Tree*. Sevenoaks: Hodder & Stoughton, 1961.

Chapter II: Feeling and Thinking

1. In Magda B. Arnold, *Feelings and Emotions*. New York and London: Academic Press, 1970, Chapter 8.
2. James Ward, *Psychological Principles*. Cambridge: Cambridge University Press, 1918.
3. Ibid., pp. 40 *et sqq.*
4. G.F. Stout, *Manual of Psychology*. Slough: University Tutorial Press, 1924, Book III, Part I, Chapter IV.

5. Susanne K. Langer, *Mind: an Essay on Human Feeling.* Baltimore: Johns Hopkins Press, 1967, Vol. I, p. 9.
6. Ibid., p. 21.
7. Three early exploratory papers of mine on feeling (as immediate experience), and its relations to knowing and understanding, were: 'Towards realistic psychology', *The Journal of Philosophy*, Vol. XXI, No. 18 (1924); 'Knowledge and feeling', *Psyche*, Vol. V, No. 2 (1924); 'Immediate experience: its nature and content', *Mind*, Vol. XXXIX (n.s.), (1930), pp. 154–74.
8. Ibid. *The Journal of Philosophy* (1924) and *Mind* (1931) for the two most significant.

Chapter III: Kinds of Knowing

1. Bertrand Russell, *Problems of Philosophy.* Oxford: Oxford University Press, 1967.
2. R.S. Peters, 'The education of the emotions' in R.F. Dearden, P.H. Hirst and R.S. Peters (eds.), *Education and the Development of Reason*, London: Routledge & Kegan Paul, 1972, p. 473.
3. A.R. Lacey, *Dictionary of Philosophy.* London: Routledge & Kegan Paul, 1976.
4. Louis Arnaud Reid, *Knowledge and Truth—an Epistemological Study.* London: Macmillan, 1923.
5. Michael Polanyi, *Personal Knowledge.* London: Routledge & Kegan Paul, 1958, pp. 196–7.
6. P.H. Hirst, 'Literature and the fine arts as a unique form of knowledge', *Cambridge Journal of Education* (Michaelmas Term 1973), p. 119, and 'Human movement, knowledge and education', *Journal of Philosophy of Education*, Vol. 13 (1979), p. 102. (An—unfortunately delayed—reply of mine appeared in the *Cambridge Journal of Education* (Michaelmas Term 1974). Another article from me, 'Art: knowledge-that and knowing-*this*' (on the same general theme), was published in *The British Journal of Aesthetics*, Vol. 20, No. 4 (Autumn 1980).)

Chapter IV: Propositional Statements, and Knowing in the Arts

1. P.H. Hirst, 'Literature and the fine arts as a unique form of knowledge', *Cambridge Journal of Education* (Michaelmas Term 1973), p. 118.
2. Ibid., p. 120 and passim.
3. Ibid.
4. William Empson, *Seven Types of Ambiguity.* London: Chatto & Windus, 1949.

5. David R. Olsen, 'The role of the arts in cognition', *Art Education* (US), Vol. 36, No. 2 (March 1983), p. 36.
6. P.H. Hirst, 'Human movement, knowledge and education', *Journal of Philosophy of Education*, Vol. 13 (1979), p. 102.
7. Ibid.
8. Ibid.
9. Ibid., pp. 102–3.
10. Ibid., p. 103.
11. Ibid.
12. Harold Osborne, 'The language metaphor in art' and Leslie R. Perry, 'The arts judgement and language', *Journal of Aesthetic Education*, Vol. 18, No. 1, Spring 1984, pp. 9–33.
13. Harold Osborne, op. cit.
14. Ibid.
15. Ibid.
16. Ibid.
17. Leslie R. Perry, op. cit.
18. Ibid.
19. Ibid.
20. Ibid.
21. Ibid.

Chapter V: Understanding Art

1. Carl R. Hausman, *A Discourse on Novelty and Creation*. The Hague: Martinus Nijhoff, 1975, p. 11.
2. Carl R. Hausman, 'Eros and agape in creative evolution: a Peircean insight', *Process Studies* (US), Vol. IV, No. 1 (Spring 1974), especially pp. 14–17.
3. Carl R. Hausman, 'Criteria of creativity', *Philosophy and Phenomenological Research*, Vol. XL, No. 2 (December 1979), p. 245.
4. Carl R. Hausman, 'Intradiction: an interpretation of aesthetic understanding', *Journal of Aesthetics and Art Criticism*, Vol. XXII, No. 3 (Spring 1964), pp. 249–50.
5. Donald Francis Tovey, *Forty-Eight Preludes and Fugues by J.S. Bach for Pianoforte*. London: Associated Board of the Royal School of Music (n.d.).
6. Ibid. Introduction to Prelude 11 of Book I.
7. René Wellek, *Concepts of Criticism*. New Haven, CT and London: Yale University Press, 1963. The chapter, 'The crisis of comparative literature', is particularly relevant.
8. I have developed the idea of 'meaning-embodied' mainly in three books: *A Study in Aesthetics* (London: Allen & Unwin, 1931; see index entries 'embodiment' and 'expression'); *Ways of Knowledge and Experience* (London: Allen & Unwin, 1961; particularly pp. 46–56 and Part I passim);

and *Meaning in the Arts* (London: Allen & Unwin, 1969, passim, but particularly Part I and Chapter 11).

Chapter VI: Understanding Persons

1. Michael Polanyi, *Personal Knowledge*. London: Routledge & Kegan Paul, 1958, p. 347.
2. Martin Buber, *I and Thou* (trans. Walter Kaufman). Edinburgh: T.S.T. Clark, 1970.
3. Frances Berenson, *Understanding Persons*. Brighton: Harvester Press, 1981, p. 105.
4. Ibid., p. 114.
5. Ibid., p. 132.
6. Ibid., p. 147.
7. Louis Arnaud Reid, *Ways of Knowledge and Experience*. London: Allen & Unwin, 1961.
8. Edward Lee Thorndike, *Psychology and the Science of Education*, selected writings ed. Geraldine M. Jarcich. New York: Teachers College, 1962.
9. Michael Polanyi, op. cit., pp. 201–2.

Chapter VII: Moral Understanding and Moral Action

1. Bernard Williams, *Moral Luck*. Cambridge: Cambridge University Press, 1981, especially pp. 30–9.
2. J.S. Mill, *Utilitarianism, Liberty and Representative Government*, London: J.M. Dent & Sons, 1910.
3. Iris Murdoch, *The Sovereignty of Good*. London: Routledge & Kegan Paul, 1970.
4. W.D. Ross, *The Right and the Good*. Oxford: Oxford University Press, 1930, p. 7.
5. Louis Arnaud Reid, *Creative Morality*. London: Allen & Unwin, 1937, p. 78. Here I refer to H.A. Prichard's *The Theory of Morals*; his essays and lectures were later gathered together in *Moral Obligation* (Oxford: Clarendon Press, 1949).
6. H. Sidgwick, *The Methods of Ethics*. London: Macmillan, 1922.
7. J. Rawls, *A Theory of Justice*. Oxford: Oxford University Press, 1972.
8. L. Kohlberg, *The Philosophy of Moral Development: Moral Stages and the Idea of Justice*. London: Harper & Row, 1981.
9. R.M. Hare, *Moral Thinking: its Levels, Methods and Point*. Oxford: Oxford University Press, 1981, Preface, p. v.
10. Ibid., pp. 44–5.
11. Ibid., p. 45.
12. Ibid.

13. Ibid., p. 46.
14. Ibid.
15. Renford Bambrough, *Moral Scepticism and Moral Knowledge*. London: Routledge & Kegan Paul, 1979.
16. J.L. Mackie, *Ethics: Inventing Right and Wrong*. Harmondsworth: Penguin Books, 1977.
17. Renford Bambrough, op. cit., p. 76.
18. Nicolai Hartmann, *Ethics*, trans. Stanton Coit. London: Allen & Unwin, 1932, Vol. II, pp. 30–3.
19. John Wilson, 'A reply to Francis Dunlop' in D.B. Cochrane, et al. (eds), *The Domain of Moral Education*. New York: Paulist Press, and Toronto: Ontario Institute for Studies in Education, 1979, p. 183.
20. R.S. Peters, 'The place of Kohlberg's theory in moral education', *Journal of Moral Education*, Vol. 7, No. 3 (May 1978), pp. 147–57.
21. Charles Bailey, 'Morality, reason and feeling', *Journal of Moral Education*, Vol. 9, No. 2 (January 1980), pp. 114–21.
22. J.O. Urmson, 'Saints and heroes' in A.I. Melden (ed.), *Essays in Moral Philosophy*. Seattle: University of Washington Press, 1958.
23. R.M. Hare, op. cit., pp. 198 sq.
24. Elizabeth Pybus, 'Saints and heroes', *Philosophy*, Vol. 57, No. 120 (April 1982).
25. Ibid., p. 193.
26. R.M. Hare, op. cit., p. 201.
27. Ibid., pp. 203–4.
28. Elizabeth Pybus, op. cit., p. 195.
29. Ibid.
30. Dorothy Emmet, *The Moral Prism*. London: Macmillan, 1979.
31. Ibid., pp. 115 sq.
32. Ibid., p. 6.
33. Louis Arnaud Reid, *Creative Morality*. London: Allen & Unwin, 1937.

Chapter VIII: Education and Ways of Understanding—Intellectual, Religious, Moral, Aesthetic

1. Millard Clements, 'Performance based education: a social alchemy', *The Educational Forum*, Vol. 46 (Spring 1982), pp. 315–16.
2. Ibid., p. 317.
3. P.H. Hirst and R.S. Peters, *The Logic of Education*. London: Routledge & Kegan Paul, 1970.
4. R.F. Dearden, P.H. Hirst and R.S. Peters (eds), *Education and the Development of Reason*, 3 vols. London: Routledge & Kegan Paul, 1972.
5. P.H. Hirst, *Knowledge and the Curriculum*. London: Routledge & Kegan Paul, 1975.

6. Michael Polanyi, *Personal Knowledge*, op. cit.
7. J. Passmore, 'Teaching to be critical', in R.F. Dearden, P.H. Hirst and R.S. Peters (eds), op. cit., pp. 25 sq.
8. Ibid., p. 28.
9. Ibid., p. 30.
10. Ibid., p. 33.
11. Louis Arnaud Reid, *Ways of Knowledge and Experience*. London: Allen & Unwin, 1969; *Preface to Faith*, London: Allen & Unwin, 1939; *The Rediscovery of Belief*, London: The Lindsey Press, 1945.
12. P.H. Hirst, 'Morals, religion, and the maintained school', in P.H. Hirst, *Knowledge and the Curriculum*, op. cit.
13. For example: John Wilson, *Approach to Moral Education*, Oxford: Farmington Trust, 1967; John Wilson, 'Moral education and the curriculum' in Monica Taylor (ed.), *Progress and Problems in Moral Education*, Windsor: N F E R Publishing (now N F E R-Nelson), 1975; Peter McPhail, 'The Schools Council Moral Education Projects', *Ideas* (University of London Goldsmiths' College), No. 28 (June 1974).
14. Gilbert Ryle, 'Can virtue be taught?', in R.F. Dearden, P.H. Hirst and R.S. Peters (eds), op. cit., pp. 44–57.
15. Ibid., pp. 51–2.
16. Ibid.
17. Ibid.
18. Richard T. Kelsall, 'Towards critical study in the primary school', and John Steers, 'The structure and content of art teaching in the secondary school', *Journal of Art and Design Education*, Vol. II, No. 1 (1983), pp. 49–80.
19. Richard T. Kelsall, op. cit., pp. 49–60.
20. John Steers, op. cit., pp. 61–80.
21. Anthony Dyson, 'Art history in schools: a comprehensive strategy', *Journal of Art and Design Education*, Vol. I, No. 1 (1982), p. 128.
22. Ibid.
23. Ibid., pp. 128–9.
24. Ibid., pp. 130–1.
25. Robert Hughes, *The Shock of the New*. London: B B C Publications, 1980.
26. Henri Bergson, *Time and Free Will* (trans. F.G. Pogson). London: Allen & Unwin, 1910; *Creative Evolution* (trans. A. Mitchell). London: Macmillan, 1911.

Index

Abbs, Peter 3, 5
abstractions, their release and their
limitations 7–9
acquaintance knowledge and
descriptive knowledge 27
aesthetic
education: 140–1; and the arts
126–38; content 129–30;
distinguished from, though
related to, the arts 129–32;
importance of body in 126–7
embodiment versus statements 40–
1
knowledge and experience 42–3
as model for educative learning
114–17
and propositional use of language
38–42
agape
Duty and duties 104–106
and eros: and art-creation 53–4;
and reciprocal personal
relationships 75–6
Alexander, Samuel, 18, 34
'archangel'
as apotheosis of reason 88
and the 'prole': why it is a
misleading metaphor 89–90
'Archangel and the prole' (Hare) 88–
90
Aristotle 89

Arnold, Matthew 41
art
children's, confusion about 131–2
direct experience necessary in 39
and dispositional knowledge 46
education 140; continuity in 133–4,
140; in primary school 132–3;
requirements 138; in secondary
school 133–4; visual 130–4, 140
as embodiment of value 40–1
and enjoyment 38, 137–8
and expression 64–5
history of: archaeological interest
in, distinguished from artistic
interest in 136–7; in curriculum
134–6; and history 136–8;
misconceptions about 134;
practical teaching of in school
135–6
knowledge of: and intuition 29; and
propositional view 32, 38–49
(Hirst, 38–46)
as new creation 51–5
and occurrent cognition 45–6
and symbols 62–5
understanding 50–65
artist, responsibility of 54
artistic
meaning—embodiment and
expression 63–5, 126–7
and scientific intelligibility 50–5

149